WITHDRAWN

Gramley Library
Salem Academy and College
Winston-Salem, N.C. 27108

House on Fontanka

Other books by Earl S. Braggs

Walking Back from Woodstock
Anhinga Press, 1997

Hat Dancer Blue
Anhinga Press, 1993

Hats
Linprint Press, 1989

House on Fontanka

earl s. braggs

ANHINGA PRESS, 2000
TALLAHASSEE, FLORIDA

Gramley Library
Salem Academy and College
Winston-Salem, N.C. 27108

Copyright © Earl S. Braggs 2000

All rights reserved under
International and Pan-American Copyright Conventions.

No portion of this book may be reproduced in any form without
the written permission of the publisher, except by a reviewer,
who may quote brief passages in connection with a review
for a magazine or newspaper.

Front cover watercolor
Daud Akhriev – *View from the St. Petersburg Studio of Piotr Fomin*

Front cover transparency – Ruth Grover
Back cover photograph – Mark Wood
Cover design, book design and production – Lynne Knight

Library of Congress Cataloging-in-Publication Data
House on Fontanka by Earl S. Braggs – First Edition
ISBN 0938078-65-8
Library of Congress Cataloging Card Number – 00-101314

*This publication is sponsored in part by a grant from the Florida Department of State,
Division of Cultural Affairs, and the Florida Arts Council.*

Anhinga Press Inc. is a nonprofit corporation dedicated wholly
to the publication and appreciation of fine poetry.

For personal orders, catalogs and information write to:
Anhinga Press
P.O. Box 10595
Tallahassee, FL 32302
Web site: www.anhinga.org
E-mail: info@anhinga.org

Published in the United States by Anhinga Press, Tallahassee, Florida.
First Edition, 2000

Acknowledgments

Natalya Strelnikova (wife)
for translating the trip into a *House on Fontanka.*

Anastasiya (daughter)
for taking her first steps at nine months in Russia.

Lynne Knight
for patience and dedication to the project.

Rick Campbell
for guidance and support of the project.

Helga Kidder
for typing, typing, and retyping each poem until we got it right.

Lavinia Johnston
for making the publication of this collection possible.

Mark Wood
for having the photographer's eye to imagine.

Daud Akhriev
for allowing me to use
View From the St. Petersburg Studio of Piotr Fomin
for the cover design.

Melissa Hefferlin
for suggesting the cover design.

University of Tennessee at Chattanooga
for the summer fellowship in 1998
that supported the writing of this book.

*The publication of this book is supported
by a generous donation from Lavinia L. Johnson*

*For Natalya
and Anastasiya*

Gramley Library
Salem Academy and College
Winston-Salem, N.C. 27108

Contents

Three

Foreword

Perhaps, as I reflect back, this trip began when I was a kid, wandering the shelves of the Wilmington, North Carolina, downtown library. It was in that place that I, somehow, came face to face with *We the Russians.* Quite an ordinary book then, an extraordinary book now. Toward the center is a photograph simply called *School Children at Red Square.* Now as I look back, I am reminded how I wished to be framed in their famous moment. But I was a Negro in a country that never cared as much for me; therefore, *School Children at Red Square* seemingly served as somewhat of an invitation to be.

Sometimes, while searching, we come upon things that define. Recently, again, I discovered *We the Russians.* Still ink stamped blue in the back is the unfaded date due: 6-17-68. To my surprise, I never returned it. Did I forget or was it my childish intent to take what was not mine? In all sincerity, I do not know. All I know is after thirty-two years, those school children are still standing at Red Square.

So I would go to Russia using the book as my passport. I would remember Langston Hughes' trip to Russia and the Negro in the American South movie, intended but never made. I would remember Claude McKay's speech to the Com-Intern and the book of essays America refused to publish. I would remember it all in the lack of lines on the faces of children.

"First there were the Russians," Hemingway said. He was talking about attention to language. As a kid, listening to Pushkin's *Fairy Tales,* somehow I must have known as much. Which reminds me of the other Russia that I remember. The six o'clock nightly news television image of Nikita pounding his fist, telling all America, "We will bury you." I remember the fear of a red Cold War, but I was never afraid of the cold or the color. I was in love with the image of the children.

But children grow and I grew up to find my love had also grown into the profile of Anna Akhmatova sitting quietly on the banks of the Black Sea, telling me she would meet me in Leningrad, Petrograd, St. Petersburg, the city of too many names, too many rivers, and too much rain. So I went and as promised just as quietly she came. At her house on Fontanka River in the First Room, there's a guest book. On its pages, to her, I wrote a long letter. From the First Room to the Last Room, I touched things not to be touched in museums. I sat at the desk where she wrote *Poem Without A Hero,* ate bread at the table where she dined, and briefly upon her pillow I laid my head where she slept waiting for the midnight knock.

So what began as a simple photograph of school children at Red Square transcended into a Soviet passage. Weeks before my wife, five months pregnant, and I were scheduled to leave, I revisited the journeys of McKay and Hughes. It all made sense—my time was upon me. I was going to Russia to see if Pushkin was still buried in the same place. On the morning of our departure, we sat on the sofa, still, for minutes of reflection in the tradition of old Russia. In less than 36 hours, I would be standing at the edge, looking onto the vastness of the Baltic Sea. The image of children playing in the breeze would blow all about me.

— *Earl S. Braggs*
April 2000

One

Inside the house on Fontanka
Where with a bunch of keys, a lantern
the evening lassitude begins
with an out-of-place laugh.
— *Anna Akhmatova*

And This Is Spring in Russia

Birch trees come alive, groves at a time.
Two weeks ago it snowed, covered all of the East
and stopped exactly at the line, the sign,
Russia.

I crossed the bleak border at night. My wife
beside me in the back seat of a German grey car.
All the passports and visas in the world were not enough
to explain my choice of borders to cross. We entered
from Poland.

Every piece of luggage was unpacked, unpacked and
unpacked and not repacked by the searchers
of small mistakes in small print. They could not

find any wrinkles in my dark face not accounted for.
Still they, the searchers of small mistakes,
kept us waiting for, it seems, hours of small questions
that repeated themselves until the questioners became
the questions. Finally

with great hesitation the road leading to where
we were going was, of course, narrow and blacker
than any American night I remember. Some say
this road with trees on either side covered any sign
of German convoy movement between war year first
and war year last.

We drove on to the sound of death rumbling
in the branches of birch trees. No light,
except occasional headlights and even they
were somehow more frightening on dark narrow roads
when one knows the history of such scenes.

My wife leaned in to comfort me. I repacked the scatteredness
of my mind. Behind us, the road disappeared
into the promise of morning spring showers and the smell
of kindly planted flowers.

This Yellow City

Van Gogh could've been born here or Van Gogh could've
lived here or Van Gogh could've died here but he didn't
and he didn't and he did not

stop here to paint this yellow city yellow. This city
Akhmatova called a museum under an open sky painted itself
the color of open day sun light

reflects and blinds, but kindly so, on days without overcast,
days that refuse light to the stars, days without night,
white St. Petersburg in June.

This yellow city is the place and these are the streets
I now walk among the new and the old, the modern
and the forgotten, the pitiful and the promised
prayer of Peter the Great

unfolds and holds tightly upon my shoulders, an American Negro
navigates a yellow daring sea. Drown, I know I will not, still
I'm afraid to hug
the closeness of my fear. Here
in this yellow city
of my lost love. This city of rounded angles
and gold top domes, this yellow city of names, Leningrad,
Petrograd, St. Petersburg. This museum under an open sky

yellow. Her name was Alla. She waited for me but not long
enough. Now, here I walk consumed in yellow loneliness
and other things yellow unnamed.

Van Gogh could've painted the yellow lights
of Cafe Terrace here, could've lived in that yellow house
on the corner here, could've lifted his yellow hair and
cut off his left ear here, but he didn't and he didn't
and he did not
stop to stretch his canvas here to paint this yellow city yellow
I walk.

The Story of Us

For Anastasiya

And yet on these rare occasions
the magic secret of magic moments is sometimes revealed
by the way the sun rises the morning after
a night of winter rain. I did not

know it then. I was laughing, not quite enjoying
myself stranded yellow in a corner chair
in a room of too many conversations. Everything empty
until she arrived. Your mother

was wearing a winter red St. Petersburg overcoat.
I was wearing construction boots. I was rebuilding my life
I did not have enough parts to finish
the smallest of hovering small talk that seemed
to exclude and include the nothingness

until she strolled into the light. So unassumingly beautiful
no rain had fallen upon the shoulders of her coat.
The room divided into quad-quiet angles before resuming
its stagnant pose. The air was thick with promise

and though stars were not visible, I knew the dipper
had positioned itself directly above me for the evening.
Slowly as she moved around the room, my rhyme became
the rhythm of winter rain.

Her eyes found me, yet I could not leave
my yellow chair. My construction boots saw the parts
that had gone so many years missing, yet they, too,
refused to unlace in the face of promise. Like me

they, too, had been broken too many times to trust
winter rain love. That night I knew
there's no gold at the end of the rainbow. I knew
vanity has never been fair. And I knew

love at first sight is a tired, worn out, hungry phrase
but that night it felt right and it proved appropriate
the morning after our first winter rain.

So my dear Anastasiya, three years after the morning after
you took your first steps in Russia, your mother
still wears her St. Petersburg red overcoat and my boots
have long been discarded. I don't need them now.

I found the angles to build my room
in your mother's eyes that winter night of rain.

House on Fontanka

(A guided but unguarded tour)

Tragedy should not be this beautiful.
Autumn leaves, yellow and red, the last of which
are being torn from careful trees
by a careless wind. An opulent show.
An early snow in St. Petersburg.

In the distance, the voice
of the great Russian winter storm smiles.
The soft parade of kindness defines the morning.
I'd forgotten such people exist.

Akhmatova lived here amid the rains and ruins
of her city. Number 18, near Nevsky Avenue
along Fontanka. A courtyard for counts
surrounded evenly by roof-high poplar
trees, now leaves float downward
to a white covered earth. The houses, yellow
as a July sun, stand in uniform formation
as if to beckon little children,
Come out and play.
Tragedy should not be this beautiful.

Yet, here it is, more than so in this city
of Revolution, city of Winter and Summer Palaces,
city of canals, city of Great Peter.
In many ways, it is an alarming atmosphere
and yes I am here wearing my American baggy pants

and a white shirt that struggles to last
from day to day. In this place of kind exchanges
I've come to exchange places with the promise of finding
the tangent of two lives separated by language
and war. Here, the doorman is proper, the door ladies,
more than so. I had forgotten such people exist.

It should be said straight away, although
it will, I suppose, in any case become clear.
Here in this house on Fontanka, in this city of yellow
Akhmatova taught the people to live and love
poetry again. In this tired sacred house
where weak women die she lived, silently aware
of illogical consequence in the sequence of rooms.
The first room. Alone, I find myself the only one
here in this room of extra hard, hard wood floors.
For a moment I take off my shoes and feel
coolness of age and history.

And I, with no choice at all, breathe it all in.
1889, in a small cottage beside the Black Sea
Anya Gorenko decided to be born in Odessa.
The twilight of dynasty covers and hovers forcing
me into a corner of decline.

Still Romanov, but
roughly so. The hungry weeds had begun to grow
in the garden of Czars. Imperial elegance, restrained
by the mark and magic of Mad Rasputin and I,
with no choice at all, breathe it all in.

On a wall 16 painted portraits of Anya once hung,
only one of which remains reminds me
that the composer was in love with her face
in profile. My jealousy is my rage, but my rage
is not jealous; it's just that I am alone in this room.

I know, as a child, she lived near here
in the 18th century town of Pushkin. I know
the wild child became a poet in that place and I know
1910 opened to the smell of *Romantic Flowers*.

What can I say. She loved Gumilyov then, that
not so handsome man who spent his last hours
here in this room beside his once wife, a life cut

short. No more flowers, no more love in the borders.
Shot because he, Gumilyov, slept on the wrong side
of the Red dead and died a poet's death.

Wallpaper walls know the story far better
than I can tell. Above the sideboard
there's an icon *Our Lady of Kasan* and picture of a man
the caption says, Shileyko, that stubborn subtle lyric poet
who stumbled upon my love's love difficult autumns ago.

1918,
the year of Alexander Blok, the sunflower seed.
By 1921, still young, he too had played too much
with the knife. I move on, more silent than before.

The second room as the first is empty of people.
The only noise is from school children in the courtyard
below.

I know Anna Andreyevna is a chosen name
so as not to distance and disgrace the given. It is
an unpleasant explanation but her father decided
no poetess in the family. I know the grim
backdrop boundary between her two centuries spilled
into two revolutions divided by a world war and
I know when the storm of Lenin and Stalin came
to outrage itself, poet masses left and Akhmatova
alone remained.

What I don't know is how
her words were made so elegantly to disappear right here
in this room.

But according to the wallpaper, fear crossed
every threshold boldly and without question, holding
so tightly onto her bloodless white fingers, still
she refused. Oh but there is history, that old odd man

who pushed and pulled Pushkin and shot him down.
This she always knew and Mad Boy Mayakovsky knew,
that instant tragic genius shot himself. For a moment
in 1930 he forgot the yellow and red falling leaves
of poplar trees. Tragedy should not be this beautiful.

The third room, I take a swallow of vodka
from a bottle I carry to soften reality. It is me
I'm mostly afraid of, but that's a private concern.

The card table says she wrote her poems on cigarette paper,
rolled them, then smoked them until her fingers burned.
Literature in Memory, was born in this room.
In this room of forbidden composition, Lev, her son
was arrested in '33, and Punin, her third husband
was arrested in this third room in '35.

The card table says *Literature in Memory,* was born
next to the heat in this room where weak women die.
Akhmatova lived here in this room

where windows are tall and wide, where walls
could hear and paintings are little and charming
and happily contaminated. In this room where
she lived more years than necessary, she often sat
eating tin-canned fish, drinking vodka in thin sips.
I take a thick sip.

There is no picture of Comrade Stalin in the icon corner
of this room. I'm getting drunk.
Should've had breakfast, but what good would that do,
anyway. I'm just listening to what wallpaper
and tables have to say.

The fourth room is somewhat sideways, stumbling from years
or something. At an odd angle, over the bed hangs
Modigliani's drawing in thin black hard lines. Near
the opposite wall, a credenza left open with papers

and such. I touch things beyond the sign
that says, *Please Do Not* … I don't give a dime,
a Dollar, or a Kopeck. I flip a card from an unmarked deck.

I sit on the window sill because I know
she wrote every one of her poems on the edge
of something or another in this room of random—
vodka induced observation. This room of dresser drawers
that claim to still hear whispers in the dark
on a desk that served to dine upon.

Scattered observations between routine existences
and things to be done. One of easy remembrances,
a wall of recall: The early cabaret years, the Stray Dog
years, the before October years, the happy years and then
the not so lucky years. Too many to name all
of memory in this room of scattered observation between
routine existence and things to be done.

The fifth room, again clearly I see. I left the bottle
on the window sill in another room. This is the question
room. *Why is our century worse than any other?*
She wrote on cigarette paper. Resentment has terrible results,
a city reduced for a time to a single frame
from a film, a single line from a poem. *Why
is our century worse than any other?*

Nothing in common with the room of a poet
in this room of Paris porcelain and Olya's figurines.
Here where years burned, room of manuscripts
and matches, the beautiful and the bitter
ashtray, room of terrible results, room of sounds
of the Petersburg courtyard courts me into
disbelieving any of this ever happened. But

the wallpaper never lies and I am told in too many
odd and uneven ways not to ask too many questions
because I might get too many answers.

Gramley Library
Salem Academy and College
Winston-Salem, N.C. 27108

The last room
a hundred mirrors reflect her one way or another.
Into a hundred mirrors I look and see one hundred me's
standing in the middle of this crowdedly furnished
perspectus.

The weight of eyelids closed in requiem casts no shadows.
1966, Anna Andreyevna Akhmatova decided to die.
A photograph, an open coffin. At the head, the student,
Brodsky. To the left, Lev. 18 years in labor camps
for being the son of two poets and nothing more.

1966, I was 14 and I did not know I knew
her then. Now years later I stand under the roof
of a yellow house on Fontanka. The windows are open.
There is a breeze that blows in from the Gulf
of Finland.

All of Russia is enchantingly quiet.
The heavy burden of a poet is retained
in footsteps upon the faded glory on a ragged rug.

Outside, an early October snow. The leaves
yellow and red fall upon the face
of the white earth. Tragedy should not be
this beautiful.

Table at the Stray Dog Cafe

And she will be wearing her Odessa
Black Sea dress, Spanish shawl draped carelessly
careful around her shoulders.

Among all of the women she will be tallest,
most elegant, the most beautiful.

Cool and polite, the evening gentlemen will say,
Anya, how delightfully beautiful you are. But
their fantastic flattery will not touch her

long thin pure white fingers wearing
simple silver rings with opulent blue stones.

I am a Stray Dog Cafe table in this place
of dark grey corners, in the blackest of which

I sit, she sits and places the slenderness
of her arms upon my shoulders, crosses her legs
carelessly careful beneath my table cloth top

and drinks the atmosphere, the slow circles
of cigar smoke. I choke at the thought of holding
her and my breath at the same time. I am blue.

I let go. I breathe the simple straightforward sweetness
of every moment she sits ennobling everyone
and everything around her. It is without any
theatrical gestures, yet she is what makes
the Gypsy music play up and down my legs.
And I see

this goddess of thin air get up and leave my chair.
The night is, as they say, still young, but I'm
leaving too. No more work tonight for me.
I just want to be forever the king
of cafe tables in all of Russia. Perhaps

my lowliness affords, somehow, such luxury. Perhaps not.
I no longer think
of myself as merely a table at the Stray Dog Cafe.

The Women of St. Petersburg

(The ones I saw)

And for no reason at all, it is only to you
that I wish to express my incomplete gratitude

for the shortness of your noon day skirts worn
at midnight and for the absence of street lights
and avenue signs. Yes, I am lost in the thickness

of your made up faces and hair upon your legs long
as a white night sun. You, in your red shoes pumped
up as tall as they go and more. You stare at me

as if you know who I am, what I do and why
it is that I came to this yellow city. Oh legs
the distance to stars and hips, curved as crescent moons,
release me so that I might be able to see the scenery.

Bus-subway packed red head beauties, you, the women
of St. Petersburg have been assigned the duty
to light the darkness of your time and my time

here in this yellow city. Release me from my stare.
What chance do I find gazing into your unconvincing eyes.
There is little surprise in your absence of smiles.

And for no reason at all, it is only to you
that I wish to express my incomplete gratitude.

It is only to you that I do.

Tragedy and the Fairytale Prince

He conquered both time and space. They say now:
The Age of Pushkin, Pushkin's St. Petersburg …
Anna Akhmatova, 26 May 1961

Outside scattering clouds assume their position, suddenly
beneath a poetic yellow sun. There's a breeze

light like leaves blowing in from the Gulf of Finland.

Springtime turns to summer and drowns itself in a warmer shade
of even green. It's the fourteenth of June in Leningrad, Petrograd,
St. Petersburg, the city of too many rivers and too much rain.

Mayakovsky never lived here, but often he would say
to Pasternak or Tsvetaeva or Akhmatova
Boris, Marina, Anna come out sometime and visit.
In some strange way, he was thinking about Pushkin
on any afternoon after a merry walk along the waterfront.

Today in that somehow same-some strange way
Natalya and I sit here by the window at a table
for two, where the carpet is perfect Russian red,
at the Cafe of Literature and think about Pushkin
this afternoon after a merry walk along the waterfront.

The walls here are somber-sky colored to approximately
frame, quite handsomely, the age of the fairytale prince.
Some called it golden, here it is somber and silver.
They tell the story by saying what they say. The walls
say

Pushkin was somewhat of a dandy and he carried a cane.
His last supper, he had it here at this table,
by the window, for two.

Waiters here are tall unhandsome men, courteous, overly so,
dressed immaculate in black trousers and white shirts

hard pressed and never released to hear or sing
the music. So

it's mostly silent here except for ice in icewater glasses.

Yet there is much talk in this well kept clean place
where walls remember and nail-hung frames frame
the fairytaler's tale as a promise frames absolute love.
The walls say what they say

Pushkin dressed in black riding boots though quite often he walked
long stretches of day and night, alone. Many mornings
he could be seen wearing Byron's poet's shirt with cuffs undone.
He had a knack for sweet talk and sweet women
of a certain gentry. They say he was kind.

Outside the Nevsky Prospekt is steaming with new summer heat.
Crowds go as though moved mechanically by a single force. They go
as *Doctor Zhivago* with voices low. Buses do not stop at every stop.
Taxis don't stop at all. No more room in the aisle. No more
space fits into the seat.

Inside the server waves to a woman walking past and brings
to our table a bottle of Spanish red wine.
The mid-afternoon early supper eaters mostly stare
at each other, at themselves, at us, at the somber-sky
color of Pushkin's wall. From the menu we order what sounds good,
Baltic langoost steamed to perfection served with red round potatoes,
red cabbage and two red other sides

of this story told in this room like a lesson in history
lectured in a lecture hall where the professor always
wears the same red as a cardinal bow tie and horn rimmed glasses.
History is in him solid as history in an oak tree
which refuses to be told without a tree saw.

Then again it is here in this tree house that I saw-
see far less than I hear. If a tree falls in the forest

and there's no one, it makes no sound, yet there is sound
in the mere non-presence of noise. The walls say what they say

Pushkin was the father, the little boy, and the spirit ghost dancer
of Russian literature and on some restless moonless nights
the darkness sometimes reveals him, well read, well bred,
a speaker of French, a small man

sitting in a small room in a chair lighter than air,
writing *The Queen of Spades,* again at his small desk,
dancing the small dance of words. He was particular, they say
about the slant of his quill.

At our table for two the table cloth is white, the salt and pepper
shakers are silver and the napkins are red and somewhat rude.
Mine keeps falling to the floor.

On a pre-October tray, our meal is brought out. *Delectable,*
is not a word in Natalya's vocabulary. She doesn't like the sound.
She doesn't finish her lobster. Beyond delicious is mine.
The server returns to ask if everything is fine. He smiles
often but never quite out of the ordinary. Natalya smiles
as he takes away what remains. Guardedly I listen

to dishes the way dishes listen to pots, to pans.
All around us small slanted conversations appear then disappear
from faces randomly sitting at tables for more than enough,
at tables for less than expected. Across the way

the aisle curves up into the profile of a woman wearing
a summer black sleeveless dress. Her back is out. Her back
is against forgetting. Her sunglasses are atop her head,
her hair is still deliciously red but her beauty is fading
into the voice of walls. They say what they say

he had four children, he named them in rhythm:
Sashka, Mashka, Grishka, Natashka. And each of them
rode the Bronze Horse with Peter, the Bronze Horseman.
Old Russian aristocracy was in their blood.

Pushkin could trace his heritage back to the black general
who guarded Great Peter's palace gate. With such history
they say why then of Pushkin's Waterloo. Like Napoleon
he gave his promise short of the last victory.

They say it was a matter of honor.
They say his Natalya danced too often with the Frenchman.
They say he sent the letter by messenger.
They say he requested a duel. It was not the first time.
They say it was cold in the morning of a grey dumb day.
They say it was over at precisely the moment it started.
They say he was terrifyingly calm.

The server returns. Once more, too often, he smiles. Dessert?
N'et, spasee'ba! We order coffee. It comes in such a small cup.
I rush to finish, rush to listen to my own small swallows.
Natalya savors the rich blackness. She doesn't use cream.
It's been almost two years now, the day we were married.
She's five months with Anya. Anastasiya is in Russia. I wonder
if she knows

about Pushkin's aesthetic discourse concerning the price of tickets
for public performance. *At least for the children,* he would say,
let them enter for free, an account of which forms
the second subject of the fairytale. They loved him

Pasternak, Akhmatova, Tsvetaeva, Mayakovsky, Brodsky, Zabolotzky.
They loved him the way children love completely, the fairytale prince.
They loved him, yet the walls say he was hard to love
but even harder not to love. They say what they say

Pushkin had his last supper here in this room.
They say January 28th was unusual and cruel.
They say 1837 was not a good year.
They say it was a dumb grey day and earlier it had snowed.
They say the poet let fall his pistol.
They say the poet found it difficult to forget how to live.
They say the contrast was unbearable. Russian red blood

spilling onto the whiteness of snow white Petersburg snow.
They say he spoke French and a Frenchman shot him down.
They say he was terrifyingly calm.
They say the sun behind the clouds stopped in the sky
and asked him not to die but the wind blew him away.
They say it was a dumb day.

The Cafe of Literature, we're leaving now and I kiss you now
Aleksandr Sergeyevich Pushkin. I kiss you now across the years
that separate then from now. Leaving now with your tears
filling my eyes, washing the stains from my cup. The server
smiles at the tip we leave. They take American Express. *I never
leave home without it,* but I need to get rid of some rubles,
need to rid myself of a few more Kopecks. *Dahsvee Dahneeyah.*
We bid good afternoon to the server and his ordinary smile.

One last look. The walls continue to talk. I check to see
if we have everything. A happy feeling engulfs me. Perhaps
because all of my life I've been happy with so little. We're leaving
now, the Cafe of Literature. Natalya and Anya walk ahead.
Pushkin holds the door open for me.

How I Got In

(Fontanka Formal Without Invitation)

Lightly, my nights are flying apart
yet how is it, I wonder, that I live
like Radnoti so carefully honest
and silent in this silent place
that has no face, this silent night
that refuses light. So far removed
from any kind of celebration.

That was last year and the year before that.
I had not yet arrived in this city
of plain clothes people and detective love stories.

Lightly, my nights are flying apart
yet how is it, I wonder, that I awake
on your side of the bed so often nowadays.

It was in the summer, along the Fontanka
that you and I dared to glance into the distance,
into the water, into the magic that fell
upon us like stars thrown from the sky.

There is no god of these white St. Petersburg nights,
only daylight affords such luxury.
Here, too, the streets are made of sidewalks and
crosswalks and don't walks.

Here, too, the streets are rivers and givers
of things not wanted, things not needed, a party
without invitation.

But somehow occasion sometimes is exactly correct
and if the attire is somehow at the same time
proper and clean and neatly pressed

admittance is granted solely on appearance
and nothing more. That's how I go in.

The New and the Worn

On the day of my leaving, the sky is bright
and the yellowness of the buildings cast
an upward light imparting a particular outward glow
of sentimentality.

And I, the walker of yellow streets, am sentimental
yet somewhat removed from the everydayness of things.
But how quickly the weather changes into rain, into
hard harsh beating words. The fragile refinement of things

like the ignorant arrangement of streets, the rain has
come to wound.

From across the street I see them before they see me,
two Nazi skinheads. And then they see me and tell me
to kiss their beloved asses louder than rain,

*We would like to kill you today but you caught us
at a bad time, you see, it's now raining and we don't want
to get our heads wet but tomorrow if you want to come by
it will be a better time to die.*

I look down at their rainsoaked shoes, then I look at mine,
the new and the worn. The black and the white. The sky
and the wounding rain.

Goodbye to a Yellow Stucco City

Eating me instead of dining me out. Why?
I leave today less than I was when I came.
Goodbye to a yellow stucco city. I say loudly

I cannot forgive you for cheating me instead
of greeting me. And St. Petersburg I can not
forgive your yellow buildings standing shoulder
to shoulder like beautiful female soldiers ready
to shoot me for walking streets.

Oh Petersburg, you city of women in short skirts
and tall heels. I forgive you in part and
in part I can not forgive you for the price
of your tickets. I'm an American tourist, not a suitcase.

Oh Petersburg, you city of dirt beneath yellow
stucco and 18th century ruins beneath gold
covered domes. Oh city of rivers, the Neva
and Fontanka, city of white nights in June,
city of haunted nobility, city of sacred ghosts, city
of summer park benches and snow white winter, I can not

forgive the way you pushed me aside when only
I wanted to ride yellow into your sunset.

Yet, now as I leave, sad, I promise the statue of Pushkin
some day I must return to learn the meaning
of all of this.

Remembering Matthews

For Bill, 1942-1997

When last I saw him, I didn't tell him
I was going to St. Petersburg. I didn't
tell him I'd fallen in love with Akhmatova

and I didn't tell him, I needed to see
my reflection in the icy black Baltic.

That evening at his New York City apartment
decorated with classical music, he played
an opera concert, I later learned,
he had planned to attend. At the end,
the night rolled over and I was drunk

on vodka and verse and voice. Yes,
he had a beautiful one. I can hear him now
stumbling through the perfume of visiting ladies.

When last I saw him, I didn't tell him
it was the Stray Dog Cabaret I hoped to find
among the smallest of midnight tables

and light blue circles of cigar smoke. I didn't
tell him about the tragic top coat Anna
so often wore or the azure shawl she so
carefully placed recklessly over her shoulders

and I didn't tell him about the fragileness
of her sacred refinement.

That evening in his New York City apartment
decorated with impressions of the Impressionist
movement, we moved out of sync and into
rhythm and blues and magic tragic carefree laughter.

In that city that never sleeps, we slept
wide awake in his voice. Yes,
he had a beautiful one. I can hear him now
ambling from pocket to pocket of his plaid jacket.

When last I saw him, I didn't tell him
I'd fallen in love with Akhmatova. I didn't
tell him I planned to visit the wild and simple country
she refused to leave and I didn't tell him

I planned to walk the left bank of the Neva,
then through the gates of Great Peter's Summer Garden.

That evening in his New York City apartment
decorated with myth recalling Roman and Greek promise.
The last silver summer before October 1917, I
didn't tell him.

That evening, he cooked Italian pasta poetry.
He recited each boiled spaghetti string line,
each diced perfect onion, each cubed bell, each
sad spin of garlic as if he knew
when I returned from Russia with or without love,
there would be no leftovers.

The Baltic Sea

I pick up a rock and skim it across the sea
Less Than One for Brodsky.
He often came here, I am told. It is cold
and vacant and I am alone.

The collar of my breeze jacket flaps, fighting
the morning wind, then again it could be
early afternoon by now.

Out beyond the vastness, blue sky touches
blue water and sings classical blues all the way
to the shore line where waves break blue,
white, and green.

Amber – 10,000 years old – can be found here,
I am told. I pick up a rock
and skim it across the sea. *Less Than One*
for Brodsky. Dampness, coldness, and unafraidness
reaches my bones, refrigerating my unevenness.

I wish I had a scarf to wrap around
my neck like a forbidden lover. Somewhere
I know on playgrounds children are playing
but that's not what I'm saying.

What I am crying to say is this: Soon
it will be night over the icy black Baltic
and all the lights will ascend to the stars.

The evening will open its even colder door
and with heart in a paper bag, I will enter
the corner of things I know oh so well.

But my mind will still be here looking out
into the blue black blue vastness, skimming
rocks across the sea *Less Than One* for Brodsky.
Less than two for me.

Mrs. Mandelstam's Kitchen

(Where Cupboards Listen)

Despite the delicious tea dispensed from the kitchen,
all was never well again. He was silent at first.

In 1964, Joseph Brodsky was accused of having no steady job
and was sent to shovel manure near Archangel in the north
of Russia. He was silent at first. Among us

we were quiet and believed what we couldn't. Then
a remarkable transformation took place in the small kitchen.

Nadezhda brewed and Nikolay recited as Brodsky did,
building to some kind of mysterious crescendo, then

letting go like the stream whistling from the pot.
In this place where lives wait for their endings

to come crawling out away from pages of humid history,
Nikolay recited as Brodsky did. His voice thick

enough to distort his moody dark eyes, his fine featured
sensitive expression just enough, just long enough

for the tea to steep. Here now in this kitchen that keeps us
we keep thinking before drinking. This is not the whole story.

Among us no one remains brave enough to tell it all.
He was silent at first.

No One Asked About the Way I Was Dressed

Long before we hear it, another bomb will fall.
Knowing this I keep still
here among the rumors.
I have fallen in love with winter.

If we were lovers in this war torn city
would the clocks tell the low dishonest truth?
Would they tell the narrowness of yesterdays?

From a window in the rear of a yellow room
I look for patterns
of flight plans in midflight. It's midnight
and I've come back to this city.

Darkness stares from everywhere and sees everything.
In the streets where they fall they stay.
It occurs to me now that bombs dig holes
beside churches and around monuments,
that a regiment bivouacs on the Rhine,
that snipers sleep on the edge of tall buildings.

One war started here in this city.
How many nights will it take?
Vineyards run evenly along ravines.
Snow whips the wind back. Young boys carry oblique weapons.
Night stops here at stoplights. Day remembers.

The brave ones disappear before they know it.
The ones of us who are left disappear but we know it.
You and I sit somewhere in separate rooms shaking
to be together. Before we know it
another bomb will fall.

One by one I have forgotten the last of the soldier girls.
The openness of military V cut, the unzipped pleasure
of down zipping a brown skirt, I have forgotten it all,
I carry a picture of you. Olive with hair trying not to be
dark red. Beautiful.

If we were lovers in this war torn city
would we choose to love in my unsafe room or would we
choose to love in yours? Would kisses be afraid of interruption,
interrogation, the integration of parts inside a movie projector
that make black and white movies so much better when there is
no color?

Who then, among us, possesses this camera, this black and white film?
Who then, among us, frames us in this black and white war?
Who develops such photographs in milk factories and process labs?
The question of clothes is upon us.

I wear my jacket everyday blue with a velvet collar. My pants
ordinary pale yellow winter plaid, my boots brown unshined.
My nationality is often subject to suspicion and my passport passes
only on occasion it has been much easier to calculate.

No one asked about the way I was dressed
so I signed my name as the name of another.
I never asked to be the enemy. I never asked
that my courtyard be shaded by grapevines.
I asked, only, not to be identified.

If we were lovers in this war torn city
would the face of burnt-out candles give slow permission?
Would the long sounds of air raids suddenly
steal permission away? What would your father say?

If we were lovers in this war torn city
would we lock the doors of unsafe rooms?
Would we remember the fields now beneath snow?
Would the snow covered naked darkness reveal
or would the soft sweet sound of snow swallow the echoes
of bombs and trucks and tanks and children who still play
in these streets where they fall they stay?

Platoons form and march. Planes touch and go.
Helicopters hover over spilled milk. Day comes
but night does not move over.
The moon is never afraid.

If we were lovers in this war torn city
would unsafe rooms tell the unsafe secret?
Would bombs rain? Would a sky full of parachutes snow?
Would the dance come stray as a bullet
we both saw coming but decided not to move?

Between the Years of Then and When

It is not by chance that the great and tragic way
of Russian history cast a sad shadow, but
it is by chance that I would be the one

left standing underneath the smoke in this room
of Fountain House that today witnesses in a white hallway mirror
that once was magic now tragic

to not see the early cabaret years, the Stray Dog years
before October that fateful night. 1917. And how

could this mirror forget Alexander Blok's poem *The Twelve*.

Mirror, mirror, stupid mirror on the hallway wall
don't look at me and tell me you don't remember
The Wayward Tram and how they shot Nikolai Gumilyov
for speaking

of human heads being sold at the grocer's instead cabbages.

Mirror, mirror, look at me, look into my eyes and tell me
you don't remember Lev, Akhmatova's boy, his years in labor camps
because he was the son of two poets and nothing more

than a number you, now mirror, refuse to count backwards.
Someone should have broken you years ago
right between the ears not years of now and then
when in Russia there was no such thing as bad luck.

Some Called Her, Anya

(Before and after October)

She was the city. She was
Petersburg. Elegant and stray
as the graceful dog she inherited
and named Tapa. Oh hands
of the slender white nights
of June, she was 65 hand painted black line
drawings stretched clear to the moon,
an angel, goddess, poetess, whore, a nun.

She was her room, long and narrow.
A Spanish shawl draped over a divan
in a corner beside a desk she dined
between poems and poetry and revolution
and smoke and love on the window sill.

Too sad to kill the more than possible,
the more than necessary, too sad to bury
the love of watching children playing
in the courtyard of the Count. She was

the day when I was expecting a visit from a friend
and the night when nobody came and
the next morning when there was nothing to eat
but stale cigarette smoke. She was
the purity and clarity of clouds. She was
the streets, perfectly planned on the shores
of the Baltic. A young restless beautiful face
posed in profile, she was
the city, a summer white night in Petersburg.

Isn't it Good to Know Winter is Coming

(When Anna Thinks of Lev)

Too many walks through the Summer Garden. Too many
white St. Petersburg nights that particular June. Soon
October will be here, then the snow will cover
the sad news and dirt of these dirty streets.

In the evening we wrote what we wrote knowing
morning would wash words away. Knowing
every promise would be pierced by stray unforgiving bullets,
knowing silence is the enemy, not the bombs

that surely and with great certainty hit their targets.
And as with greater certainty we remember the smallness
of things, a few things, that go untouched but still
ruined like *Hello* on a sacred morning or *Good Afternoon*
past midday of a fatal week. Words leak.
Don't talk too much. Walls still listen.

In St. Isaac's Cathedral we were afraid to pray.
Breadlines did not forgive even the oldest among us. We
waited at prison gates for days with small assurances
for our loved ones. We knew nothing. We assumed, however,
if they took the package, it meant our someone
was still alive.

Why is our century worse than any other? Anna's question.
Not even God can say for sure. Anna's answer.

In every corner of the city there's war. The inside
is executing the outside even in our yellow rooms.
Walls still listen. Don't talk too much. Hope
is hallow, promise is too piercing to swallow, but
isn't it good to know winter is coming. The dead
will freeze in their graves and the smell of corpses
will dissipate in thin white air.

Leaving Vladimir

1937

With blinders on, still the eye of the horse sees
everything when everything sees nothing.
It is only natural, however, that the day before yesterday
a poet was arrested, that yesterday a poet
was executed, that today the newspaper was silent.
No incident, no situation and surrounding circumstance.

The dance continued at the club. People come lively
and go as before. Nothing has changed, snow beats
and breaks window panes, the unbearable heaviness
of death

creases us all but just a little. It is only natural,
however, we come to expect, tomorrow a poet
will be arrested. The day after a poet will be executed.
The following day the newspaper will be silent. All
will be well.

People will dance at clubs around the city. The streets
will be packed with people who hear nothing and see
even less. Fear will take cab rides to addresses
unknown and unannounced. The police will kill the police
for speaking a single line of poetry.

The young boys, then, will join the ranks of uniform
unjustice at alarming rates, more proudly than ever
and the poet will write silently in a silent room. Someone
will knock on the door at midnight, always midnight.
The future will know itself by the intonations
of heavy handedness.

And this will come with little surprise to the eyes
of the poet. His bags will be packed; he will be
prepared to leave behind all that has previously
gone unsaid, unread, unwritten, unleft in Vladimir.

View of the Obsolete

(17 minutes before 1953)

Nothing has changed.
Raindrops beat dead red drums. And on off days
snow still whips back morning room curtains and Mama calls
out loudly, *Do not forget to wear a coat.*

But we children are old enough to realize early
no wool garment is thick enough to protect
the cold of undeclared war tanks
and trucks that rumble up and down
playground avenues that may never sleep again.

The Neva streets are never more crowded
than when one is alone and afraid and little and scared
to play hide and seek. Yes, we know we will not
be found so we do not seek

the cold iron red truth. Yesterday was like a film,
an absolute obsolete foreign movie shot in slow motion
black and white and red. This morning it's twelve below
zero and falling even if I do not speak.

But I've already spoken in spite of myself. I am a Jewish boy
eight and a half years old. My mother's name is Nadezhda.
She meets her ends in a factory, melting cheeses. My father,
he lives on an ice farm in Siberia
because he wrote a poem.

Waiting for the Door

In these nights in our rooms we wait.
We are ready. We are packed. We know
'36, '37, '38 and we will never forget 1939.

Yesterday was almost normal, almost beautiful.
We heard no bad news. The day before
not so easy to digest. Not so easy to swallow.

In these nights we wait in our sad rooms
afraid to write poetic lines on unpoetic pages,
afraid the wrong eyes will read and not forgive
so we burn poems to keep warm and hope

among us, someone will remember our forgotten rhymes,
our forced line breaks, our metaphors and
similes, our preoccupation with format, our trembling
Februaries.

Stalin is a holiday we refuse to celebrate. Cut
the death cake and bury the young writer face down
after the execution in front of the wall where he stood
he fell. In these nights of careful laughter

we wait for that dreaded midnight knock. We are ready,
we are packed, we are prepared to burn the house down
but we have no more matches and the breeze has stolen
the light from the last candle.

A Wall Before Winter

(Beyond Berlin)

All along the boulevard, clouds of people collect
broken pieces of brick promise as souvenirs.
Tomorrow they may choose not to keep

pace with transit trains of falling walls
loud as thunder dust from the yellow tractors
pushing down stone gate fences

into the faces of strangers meeting
at center stage. The setting is simple,
a chair. Down the hall

my youngest daughter cries out,
Father. Her tiny voice fades
into the echoes of pitch nightness

awaking her from a dancer's dream
of falling. She takes a pencil from a crayon box
and draws a line through the center of Market Square

I pedal a silver '59 Schwinn faster, faster
without looking backwards into the eyes of Nikita
and Kennedy faced-off at Checkpoint Charlie—1961

is a long time to wait. Stop at the red sign.
My daughter erases the line. Look both ways. I ride on
into the folded arms of a rewinding town clock

clinging to the courthouse wall. Time changes
click as a bedside nightlight. The tables turn
into dancing Deutsche Marks. The year is 1930

something. I am the rumpled plaid blue boy
playing piano in the room above the parlor.
Across the street night comes to life in Cafe Josty
a rowdy ritzy crowd listens to a Radio Joe

Louis knock out the lights of Berlin City.
Then as now I can eat on the side of town I choose

the woman with red lips, red dress
and red tall shoes standing still
as a soldier. We dance slow
circles through the thick fog covering the city's eyes
lined in mascara purple as thunder.
Maybe now the rains will stop
the shiny black boots

marching between the legs of my oldest daughter
making up her face in French red rouge
while the middle girl makes up stories

about how war is a television
commercial we can choose not to buy
like soap and American cigarettes.

Earl, I wish you could see the little matchless children
crying in the background, playing hide and seek
between pages no one is willing to read.

I wish you could see the old men
carrying their mothers to the other side
hiding their torn faces behind habit.

I wish you could see
the smoldering indifference in the puzzled faces
of the young Grey Lions

looking taller than ever. I pedal on afraid to trust
the weight of my rainsoaked shoes to push me beyond
where most of my life has dared me to go.

But you know, Earl, somehow
the people are more afraid now that it's gone.
There was something safe about that wall.

Suddenly We All Grew Up

(An old Russian movie)

You and me and Y and Ze, merely boys
in the secret streets of the city of M. Slightly

sane, slightly drunken, slightly mad
to leave, slightly crazy to stay and play

childish games of hide and not go see.
You and me and Y and Ze knew so little

of the bigness of our own red history, yet
in things big and small, in school, we thought

we'd learned the definition of revolution
and the recipe of color resolution. But

wrong we were, you and me and Y and Ze never
considered the irony of bitter, beautiful death.

And somehow, oddly, somehow we must have failed
to recognize the color of color television. Now

like in a movie of war we must, you and me and Y and Ze
I suppose, head for the hills beyond the city of M

where snow drifts with or without clear purpose,
where red flows in patterns upon white unlined paper

where tragedy calls you and me and Y and Ze
to not see, that this is just an old Russian movie.

A Tragic Carnival

Sometimes a year looks back and howls then drops
To its knees.
                    Miklos Radnoti

A beautiful song had ended. August was a cruel month.
Alexander Blok was dead. The piano had stopped.

Early autumn came counting numbered days
1921, still young, depressed by a vision
Alexander Blok was dead. The last note. No encore.

Wearing a simple black suit and a wool white sweater
perhaps he should have known better
but he chose not to know better

and within the first seven days before the leaves
decided to fall, he fell

so far away from where he stood between the red
and the white, the old and the new, the civil
and the war of the heart.

He loved, I am sure of this, the way
blood can love the land of its birth, but

dark were the names unreadable at night and
at first light he was found in that place

where edges vanish and lyrics can no longer save
the last song for last. The piano had stopped.

A beautiful song had ended. August was a cruel month.

Russian Rhyme 1936

Bury me in a homespun brown labor camp suit,
shoot my friends for whispering my name.

Blame the flame on the haze and smoke—
joke played on the bitches in the black pot brew.

You, the maker of fatal lists name nine
kind reminders of Red Square scare.

Dare take off your snow coat and high hat,
cat scan a woman and a man for writing words

herds of cows, masses of so called goats,
throats bleed silently bright day red.

Dead un-understanding amasses noticed but unseen
in between frequent and always midnight door knocks.

Locks without keys, knees cracked by a black tall boot.
Shoot my friends for whispering my name.

Aim the firing squad perfect, play your death march music,
then let the people choose it.

By chance and this be it only
we dance like tomorrow who knows

better than we. You the maker of lists
name nine. Be not so unkind.

The Two Deaths of Vladimir Mayakovsky

I shall forget the year, the day, the date.
Mayakovsky

Twice before he had played Russian roulette
with himself and won.

The final version of savored verse was third
and lasted not through the morning.

April 1930 was a cruel and unforgiving month
yet it was spring time and springs are friendly.

Somebody said he killed himself over a woman.
This I do not know. But I know only odds

and ends surrounding the morning are known
and odds and ends don't make it so.

This I do know: She was seventeen, hopelessly
in love with a poet and she waited

hopelessly, for there was no return. A note
was all she wrote and that was the first.

Anyway, it was just as if or if as just
was it anyway. That's how it is, the way it goes.

The final version of savored voice was third
and lasted not through the morning.

And as mornings often do, that morning rang
its round down beneath where we all stood

waiting to hear what we came not to hear
but heard, the third and final shot

ring out all across the vastness and echo
in the ears of the *Bedbug* asleep

in his uniform complete with long black boots
and a hat covering his doubled pupiled eyes

and we, the maker of simple Russian fruit salads
were not surprised by the stage front and center

without sides, without walls or rooms just empty spaces.
A place with two holes straight through the middle

so precise, they looked like one and the same
but just as precisely aren't by any unstretched imagination.

Two

Postcards from an American
in St. Petersburg
to an unnamed woman

ВСЕМИРНЫЙ ПОЧТОВЫЙ СОЮЗЬ.
UNION POSTALE UNIVERSELLE. RUSSIE.
ОТКРЫТОЕ ПИСЬМО. - CARTE POSTALE.

Sept. 17

Tonight it rains as the last.

From O'Hare International to Carroll Street.
You'll have to take the Chi-Town Elevator train.
Across rooftops of tenement flats you'll cruise
the dense blue low ridge of square hills.

Take the Eastside Exit at the get-off station.
Allow the city to reveal itself in combinations
of traffic lights.

Love Hudson.

to an unnamed woman

untyped address

no new zip code

9

Вид от Благовещенской площади (пл. Карла Маркса) в восточном направлении.
Вверху слева Свято-Покровский монастырь,
справа – колокольня Успенского собора.

© Фирма "ЛИНОТИП" т. 47-19-16

ВСЕМІРНЫЙ ПОЧТОВЫЙ СОЮЗЪ.
UNION POSTALE UNIVERSELLE. RUSSIE.
ОТКРЫТОЕ ПИСЬМО. - CARTE POSTALE.

Sept. 18

Night rain, romance, dance, and a candle. Alone.

Tell the yellow taxi man,
"III South Michigan Ave, at Adam Street."
Take the long way, the yellow taxi man will not mind.
Stop for a moment at Sister Rosalita's Flower Shop.
Leave the meter running. Run inside.
14 Sun Flowers in a pale blue vase.
Reflect a smile upon my distant face. Pretend
for a moment you're in Amsterdam.

to an unnamed woman
untyped address
no new zip code

Love Hudson.

9

**Вид от Благовещенской площади (пл. Карла Маркса) в восточном направлении.
Вверху слева Свято-Покровский монастырь,
справа – колокольня Успенского собора.**

© Фирма "ЛИНОТИП" т. 47-19-16

Sept. 21

It has rained heavily during the past few days.

"Art Institute of Chicago, Madam." Listen
to the yellow taxi man's foreign accent.
Interrupt his foreign rear view stare.
Exit as a lady would from a horse drawn carriage.
Stop. Notice the foreign bus stop bench.
Sit for a while. Notice the foreign fancy cars
rush foreign into the afternoon. Notice twisted sister
twisted foreign in her frame of mind. Give to her
no more than one foreign American dollar bill.
Linger a bit longer before going inside.

Love, Hudson.

to an unnamed woman

untyped address

no new zip code

9

Вид от Благовещенской площади (пл. Карла Маркса) в восточном направлении.
Вверху слева Свято-Покровский монастырь,
справа – колокольня Успенского собора.

© Фирма "ЛИНОТИП" т. 47-19-16

Sept. 24

Light rain scattered evenly by the forecast.

Picasso will meet you at the door, the perfect gentleman
caller. Be courteous when you leave him talking
to himself. You'll hear a saxophone. Do not look for it.
The source cannot be identified. The impression
of colors will hesitate. Hurry, Vincent will be waiting
in a yellow room in a yellow house, silent as a picture show
you'll know.

Love Hudson.

to an unnamed woman

untyped address

no new zip code

9   Вид от Благовещенской площади (пл. Карла Маркса) в восточном направлении.
Вверху слева Свято-Покровский монастырь,
справа – колокольня Успенского собора.

© Фирма "ЛИНОТИП" т. 47-19-16

Sept. 29

Raining sheets and night colored lace.

The discontinuity of Poliakoff's paint may set aside   to an unnamed woman
the stated pattern of your softest approach.   untyped address
Leave Serge be.   Leave Camille be.   no new zip code
Too dull to see "A View of Malakoff"
beneath the unnaturalness of studio light.
Leave them all be: Henri Rousseau, Mary Cassatt,
Frida Kahlo, Masolino, Bernardo Bellotto.
Say hello as you leave.   Leave them all be.

Love Hudson.

9

Вид от Благовещенской площади (пл. Карла Маркса) в восточном направлении.
Вверху слева Свято-Покровский монастырь,
справа – колокольня Успенского собора.

© Фирма "ЛИНОТИП" т. 47-19-16

ВСЕМІРНЫЙ ПОЧТОВЫЙ СОЮЗЪ.
UNION POSTALE UNIVERSELLE. RUSSIE.
ОТКРЫТОЕ ПИСЬМО. - CARTE POSTALE.

Oct. 1

It's raining again.

Stand in a vacant corner. Count the steps you take
stopping at seventeen. You'll notice
Vincent's space will light in unusual yellow bright.

"Cafe Terrace at Night" 1888.
Facing the master and the masterpiece
undress for me as you stroll the rain of a Paris Night.
I have come to love the color.

Love Hudson.

to an unnamed woman

untyped address

no new zip code

9   Вид от Благовещенской площади (пл. Карла Маркса) в восточном направлении.
Вверху слева Свято-Покровский монастырь,
справа - колокольня Успенского собора.

© Фирма "ЛИНОТИП" т. 47-19-16

58

Three

… I suppose that at first, it was people
who invented borders and then borders
started to invent people.
                    — *Yevgeny Yevtushenko*

The City of Yes and the City of No

For Yevtushenko and Bella

My love is a yellow taxi cab rushing
for weeks now between the city of Yes and the city of No.

Either or neither of which I go open heartedly.
It is, I'm afraid to say, even more so today,

the city of Indecision that comforts me in cabs
of so little beyond naked honest contemplation.

The city of Yes where wild beautiful horses roam
across wide openness in corners of southwest hearts

and then there's the city of No where even the brave
ones dare ride to break the wild into small even pieces.

It is safe here in the city of No. Everyone
goes and comes about business quite ordinarily.

But in the city of Yes, the call of the wild calls
clear as a name, *Come on over tonight.*

Bring a bottle of wine, we'll start a fire below the mantle
of things we choose not to mention in daylight.

The city of Yes, the city of No. The city
of Indecision is pointless precision and nothing more.

The city of Yes where buildings are intimidating
and the city of No where they are not quite so.

Once you go to the city of Yes, you can never
ever go back to the city of No. But

like Nabakov and his battle with butterflies,
I see how beautiful things could be

in the city of Yes and yes the city of Yes
is tragically peaceful when she speaks of the moth.

Listen, let me explain something to you. It was, I think,
at a side street cafe that I first saw her, then

again at a small corner coffee house I most often passed
on my way home. For no apparent reason I stopped

one afternoon. Between us, there was no conversation.
Between us, there were no stares, no stars, yet I felt magic.

Just as quick, I finished my cup and left. She savored
hers and stayed. Magic followed me home.

My random routine, she must have found while searching
for random meanings of running into each other

so often, I've wondered if I believed
the pure white beauty of her hands quicker than my eyes.

I must say for a while I noticed little until
she started showing up between the words on my poet's page,

dressed as if waiting for a part in a made for TV movie.
Always, she knew her lines, would speak them and leave

always as I entered. Yes, I believe in moments
without preposition, I believe in questions

without question marks and I know adjectives can't explain
everything but somehow I forgot how to write

simple paragraphs with simple transitional devices
and started anticipating her random arrivals.

For weeks now between the city of Yes and the city of No
my love is a yellow taxi cab rushing through rush hour

traffic. The city of Indecision where the rent is too high.
The meter keeps running. The driver keeps talking in a foreign language.

I do not want to understand. It's raining in both
the city of Yes and the city of No.

The sky is dark, cold and calling for snow.
People hug tightly the winter lining of fur coats,

but my view from either window of my yellow taxi
is the simple ordinary beauty of wild running horses.

Hey Mister

(The fugitive blue of color)

Second of all,
it isn't necessary for me to remember now.
The battleships have sailed for Odessa, I am not aboard.
I have dried my salty hair in the air
of a bigger sky. I needed to die, tell her.

And Sir, when you see her, compliment her
about the way she looks. Tell her the cling
is a bit too red but nice as any autumn rose.
Yes, I've twisted myself to praise but not promise.

I've given to sitting in windows and watching
flames leap blue, orange, and beautiful,
to listening to the pop of hot green wood burning.
I've given to taking my days more slowly now. Tell her

it's an off centered scene in between too many maybe nots
and maybe's. In between the cut of wedding cakes
sliced into celebration, opening ceremonies. Tell her
she looked good the other day when I saw her
at the dedication. It isn't necessary for me to remember
now

Tell her, Sir, for me, if you will,
not to wear her complexion too tight
at night when it rains. Tell her not to turn unread pages
too rapidly against the wind, and Sir, tell her
not to pull the colors from leaves before they fall.

Everyone needs a rake, the kind when you step on it,
it hits you in the face. It wakes you up differently
from the soft alarm clock music
now sleeping beside my bed. I must have read
too many ghost stories as a child. Tell her to dial
my number and let it ring forever. Tell her
there is always more than should be said.
I was dead, tell her

my sleep was lulled by too many return addresses,
too many airmail letters unmailed, too many stamps
commemorating famous people in too many boxes
in too short a period of time for anyone to know
where I lived. It isn't necessary
for me to remember now, the size of envelopes.

Mayakovsky's *Bedbug* on top of the radio
and I have turned the volume way down low. I know
the difference between papier maché and paper maché
promise, tell her.

Until pointless, I suppose I could go on telling you
about the slow move of battleships, about the cling of red leaves,
about the fit of black market shoes, but I save the speech
I might have made.

Which way she comes, it matters little. What time,
what day, whatever. I will not be waiting.

Hey Mister, tell her this
first of all.

Akhmatova Said

For Yesterday's Girl

Akhmatova said, *I shall come back*
in your dreams as a black Ewe.
I say, I shall come back by the same name,
softly into your dreams as I was before.

Lately, you've painted me as a portrait
you don't know when all the time you know
me as I know you. The rain people we are
born under the name sign. The moon.

Soon is what I try to believe in, but it moves
seemingly away from me in this room
with too many windows to look from,
this room that still struggles to be named.

What? Is the big question that I've given name to
in between these winter sheets and nights,
sleeping alone. In spite of all I now feel,
this I know to be true.

The names of stars come out for you
even on rainy nights and we can still sit outside
'til the sun, counting names one by one.
And if one falls, I'll find it for you.
I know where the names of rain stars fall.

I could name all the parts of your face
that I love in one long paragraph, name conjunctions
together that will not break, write sentences
without verbs and not be afraid

that you will ever forget my name.
A storm could rain — name oceans into the sea
and not wash away my name. Akhmatova said,
You will hear thunder and remember me.

The Dance of Birch Trees

For Anna Andreyevna Akhmatova

And your face, as it was then, will be beautiful.
Years later, the trees, they tell the story
all too differently. Yet

it is here that I remember the art
of hand-tailored elegance, savoring cigars
on late winter afternoons.

Waiting, we waited and waited
until we were what we must have wanted to be.

Years later, the trees, they remember, I suppose
the casual gallantry of long walks
along the wide streets of Great Peter's city.

Yes, it is how I wanted to dance with chance
in the rain-wet curls of your hair that mattered most,
but most, most often doesn't really matter,
does it?

Now, yet, it is here that I find the time
to recall it all, covered by the way you laughed

and how you listened so intently to everything
I said and did not say but said anyway.

Therefore, it is with some excitement
that I look back to see how years later, the trees
have captured my mind in the cages

of softly written sentences that stand securely
without verbs or prepositions. Nothing but
adjectives too exact to describe the simple slow dance
of birch trees.

After all these years, years later, my hope,
is to remember the way they sway in stopless wind
and your face, as it was then, will be beautiful.

Table for Cards

You say you like old Russian movies
with yellow subtitles never white. I say

Doctor Zhivago in Russian was never made.
You say *So!* I think of the word *us*.

And now we're sitting here at a table
for cards in this room of chance, romanticizing

about a movie unmade. You are smoking.
You haven't stopped yet. You are beautiful

in the way you smile so often. It's been seven weeks now
since I first met you for coffee

and we haven't made love yet. We are waiting
for the summer solstice. You're funny that way.

I know that. I know you are married.
I know I am not, but once I was. I know

you have no promises. I know I keep them like I keep
secrets, not long at all and I know seasons change

but what I don't know is what hand, if any,
you are going to play. Four of a kind I'm guessing,

four aces or four deuces, nothing wild, a straight poker face.
The fifth card doesn't matter at all. I fold,

I fall. No ace, no king, no queen, no jack, no 10
in the same suit I've been wearing seems like forever

is quite long enough with the right sound track
we could take everything said all back and I'll be

the leading man in a winter Russian movie
we could make tonight on or at this table for cards.

A Letter to Akhmatova

(From me)

Dear Anna: Here now it is winter
and I keep trying to bring back things.
The forecast is calling for flurries. All and all
today is beautifully sad. I am haunted,
of course, by memory. Yet how is it I wonder

that I find such comfort in your voice.
For the first time in years, I am here alone
in a winter room without drapes. Outside

the beautiful and the sad decorate and alternate
side by side and birds scribble language into snow
none of which I can read. I need patience
I suppose and I suppose everything goes

toward something. I spent my Kopecks on flowers
for you. When the forest burned, you were the one
that chose not to leave your country. And I
was the one who stayed there beside you to hold
your fragile white fingers. I, too, was burned
beyond recognition.

Oh, Russia with your long hair cropped by blaze,
raise my patience for me. Dear Anna Gorenko,
bring to me your Black Sea, let me live
in your Odessa, give me your voice,
your photograph in profile, and I'll learn to understand
that patience is the last thing we learn.

How to Unwind this Merry-go-round

For Bella Akhmadulina

Around and around and around and around we go
at a pace that distorts the face. Where to stop?
I do not know, but Bella does

this evening down at the club, she recites from memory
Fifteen Boys, maybe more, maybe less. Some
precariously perched on window sills. Some
have taken seats in the aisle

while, nonchalantly, she strolls from stage center
to stage right bringing together two ends of one night

into the spotlight. Glamour against a dense backdrop
she drops line by line, one at a time. *Fifteen Boys,*
maybe more, maybe less. Some
front and slightly off center. Some
yell from the way-back row. She is wearing a black dress,
silk and short, explosive like a volcano with reddish hair.

Leave, none would dare. Stay, even if they have to pay.
Fifteen Boys, maybe more, maybe less. Some
want it fast. Some
want it slow. I do not know, but Bella does.

Why? Partly I Suppose

And then there's the great pleasure of long letters
from would be former lovers, fancy girls

or from an old flame still with an old smoldering fire
not quite warm enough for winter in this place.

Now that the snow has melted, morning finds me
here, alone where white nights whisper

oh so softly I've slept for years in the remembered
passion of your arms. I once dreamed of horses

wild, running across the clear blue day of a great plains
and must have awakened with you on my mind.

Why? Partly I suppose I've been exacerbated
by vague rumors of your return to this city

beyond promise and partly I suppose I've been wounded
by too many white winters, too many white promises.

According to Akhmatova, winter is by far
the oldest of seasons. According to me is according to snow.

Now I know why. Partly I suppose
that's the way love comes and the way loves goes.

Perhaps We Will Learn

If we never made love the horses
would never have to die and we could
ride them gracefully

wild and carefree on summer afternoons
across the wide open desert plains where the sky
touches the goldenness of the sand. If

we never made love the horses would run
forever against the azure. But
we made love and now we must face
the slaying of Promise and Purpose, the names

of horses we've given to taking things not so lightly
now as we walk away separately concerned
with the choice we've made out of love. And

on some cool foreign afternoon perhaps we will learn
to paint horses upon the canvas again. Promise
and Purpose running against the azure. And

if magic can somehow find her moment perhaps we, too,
can find life again in the colors of simple paint.

Girl on a Painted Horse

I could begin by telling you I'm in love with her.
I could tell you happiness is a lot like playing
hide-now-go-seek and find an unmiserable corner
in which to sleep. I could tell you this is my room
and these are my promises, but I won't.

What I will tell you is this: Every day she's there
on that same corner of the morning. Every day
I walk by. She laughing or smiling most often

but today it appears she's been crying someone else's tears.
Not possibly her own. She's such a happy girl
on her painted horse. Yeah, I know I could ask why
but just like yesterday and the day before, I walk by.

Her horse was painted by crazy Picasso, I overheard
someone say. And she used to hang quite handsomely
in a gallery on Society Street, but that was before
she started hanging out here

down at the local Bar and Grill, pretenders kill
to talk to her. But me, I don't want to talk,
I want to ride her painted horse like a cowboy,
right through an alley of gunslingers blazing
from every direction. Like a Navajo, I'll be naked
in the saddle through a herd of cattle. But
that's another story too.

In the quiet of the day I say to myself. Yellow
ain't no color to paint a horse. Why Picasso?

Why not green like Kandinsky? Blue like Monet?
Pale like Goya? Silver like Cezanne? Free
like Frida Kahlo? Pink like Jackson Pollock?
Belloto, Michelangelo, El Greco?

Van Gogh would know. I go, some days, to places
I've never been before and she's always there

yellow as the Amsterdam sun and she's always riding
away from where I'm going and that would be okay
if I could turn around but I can't.

It's too early in the morning. I haven't had my coffee.
I need a whole pack of cigarettes to get me through this.

I miss the curtain and I miss the call
to be a painter, but this ain't no play on words.
This is my life and she's a picture in a frame,
that's all. And I could end by telling you I'm in love with her
but I won't.

But She Never Did

Inside, I must say, I waited, then
outside, I went to smoke a cigarette, then
inside again, to wait longer, to wait more.

Sad, my choice, this I know, yet
it must be said that I enjoyed
parts of my impatience, the notice
of small children playing fox and rabbit
games between interruptions.

The whole station
was something from a movie house, unproduced
and undirected. Yet, there was direction
in the coming and going of buses.

From the other direction, at last she came
at least for a moment I thought
but then I saw she turned out to be
only a woman with similar eyes and
a similar gait. To wait, yes, I continued, but
in those similar familiar eyes.

She was, this woman,
extremely cordial with a certain warm dignity,
an overglow about herself that kept my attention
far longer than I anticipated.

Perhaps to wait is like counting concentrically,
the smaller the circle, the larger the comedy
of error.

Perhaps to be sandwiched between two cities
in a bus station makes the wait obsolete.

Perhaps to fall so completely into the eyes
of another softens the perception of my
own sadness or

perhaps the subject of my wait found out
in the middle of the morning what
I intended to say to her later today.

Perhaps not. The deepness of green eyes left
and I fell. Buses continued to come and go.
The children changed the name of the games
they played and my wait waited

for my impatience to catch up again.
Another cigarette, another cold outside, cold hard
waiting seat, another sun but the same wakeless moon.

In Which Language Do I Keep Silent

For Cathie, the modern dancer's moon

I know that if a number is raised to the first power, the exponent
is usually not written. I know that the absolute value of a number
is that number without its sign. Without a sign, there's no way to tell
who I am. Today I will not give any indications. I know that

the angular velocity of your movement is too beautiful to name
and I've come to recognize you as a dancer in lines of my own poetry.

It's a funny thing how books can be read upside down and maps
get us most lost. I know this from experience. Lately,

I find myself looking at maps, measuring distances between cities.
One inch equals twenty-five miles. $1/25$ of one inch equals one mile.
Small towns are represented as dots. I question the mathematics of it all.

My whole numbers have become fractions on a November calendar.
I've learned to count parts of each square. I know what it's like
to have nothing but time.

The night I first saw you dance, I followed the softness of your steps
across the floor, across the studio, every spin taken into consideration,
every jump.

I know the shortest distance between us is a straight line. I want to leap
with you but not tonight because when I divide the time of day
into the time I've known you
multiplied by the number of times you've crossed my mind lately,

the answer is way too early to tell what I'm feeling. I know
the wrong answer is not always wrong.

Do you know how to tango?
Would you teach me to ride music in wide open space? Would you
teach me to dance to the unexplained, deliberate as the unexplored
dances to the patterns of treasure maps? Would you teach me
to close my eyes when I kiss?

I know the coefficient of *A* to the second power is *1*.
I know what it feels like to be alone in a room too many nights in a row.
I know how to fly without wings.

If you were a jet airplane traveling at 7.50 kmh while gaining altitude
at a constant rate, if you traveled between points 5.80 km apart,
what is the gain in altitude? I would figure it out and catch up with you,
meeting at the vertex. I know the pythagorean theorem.

Some mornings
I know my dreams lie to me to make me feel better. I laugh,
trying to figure out the ones I now have. I am not saying
I dream about you. I'm saying you are in my dreams and most often
I wake up falling.

I know the distance I fall equals ½ times the acceleration times
the time squared it takes me to fall. According to the only map

I can find tonight, my silence is one mile, ¹⁄₂₅ of an inch away
from you in either direction. I know that speed equals distance divided
by the time I sit here on this balcony, looking over the city and wait.
I know exactly how long it should take if I were to measure
your gaze in either of the two languages I now speak.

I light myself another cigarette. I don't say a thing.
I ponder the velocity of silence.

A Hundred and Thirty Suns in One Sunrise

For you, you, and you

Nevertheless, it appears that I am
exceedingly well suited to be alone
in my yellow room. I need nothing except
the freshly laundered lack of Russian explanation.

More than possible, more than necessary
I guess I've stubbornly learned to live
between expectation and the lack thereof.

Lips I might have kissed continue to visit
from time to time and I might add
that patience is the final examination
at a school I no longer want to attend

to the business of being happy. Listen you,
who have forgotten color and hue. There is love
at the borders of countries unnamed. You
would not recognize me now. I've changed
my nationality. I've taken to counting days.

A thousand ways to say, *yes, I still love you*
and I can't think of a single line.
I hear your music even when not paying attention.

Listen, you, do not play my aloneness with your
simple fiddle string. I have tossed aside,
for now at least, everything.

Tonight I Want to Write

Tonight I want to write like Pablo Neruda.
I want to fall madly and completely in love

for the very first time. I want to move
beyond the outreaches of Santiago where I know

not a single face, then trace the redness of lipstick
on a white shirt until it unzips the tenderness

of a naked skirt with plaid pleats and a promise
to spend forever together locked in silliness

like jumping rain puddles at thirty-one,
like shooting stupid cupid through the heart,

like Robin Hood with an apple on his head instead,
like carving names into the bark of an oak tree.

Tonight I want to write like Pablo Neruda.
I want to be the postman who brings your mail,

the mailman who postmarks your every letter,
the carrier who opens your mailbox even on holidays.

I want to be Christmas for you, Easter, Thanksgiving,
the Fourth of July, the fifth, the sixth, seventh, and eighth.

I want to be the seasons and months and minutes
that multiply into long days and easy weeks of pleasure

defined on the scale of commitment and contentment
in letters placed in my brown big leather bag.

Through rain through sleet through snow I want to go
from Naples to Nigeria all in one sweeping motion,

like Spain with her back against the ocean
or Portugal on a good wine day. In every way

I want to be the czar in every car on the avenue,
the president in every white house on the block.

I want to live in a room with too many windows
where the sun and moon worship the smallness of just a single bed.

And everything I will say, I've already said.
Tonight, I want to write like Pablo Neruda.

Nothing to Declare

Tall tale signs tell the time in seven different zones
on one wall. Down the hall Duty-Free is far
from being. American Tourister luggage rolls
almost without effort. Flight attendants stroll beyond
the greatest of ease. Expressionless features shuffle
toward restless gates. Everyone waits.

Near breaking point, the excitement of child's play.
Terminal noise refuses to awaken back-packed students
from another country asleep in another world. Above and slightly left,
announcements amplify the coming and goings of places

stolen from paper-made cartography: Hamburg, Germany,
Gate 6C, Frankfurt 21B, New York via New Everywhere,
Paris, France, is just a hop-skip dance away.
But I who can not dance, chance the exchange
of currency. I am entering Russia without conviction.
Rubles and Kopecks count themselves lucky. I am not
so much as.

Treading lightly the surface, my luggage
does not roll so easily. Customs is also a counter
that counts me suspicious. My baggage claim ticket
is my claim to fame, but I am not famous, I am
an American in Moscow and I am afraid

in this place where men are taller than morning and
the short black skirts of girls are indescribably
beautiful and sad. Yet

it is precisely here that I find myself facing
a sign – Passport Control Conveyor Belt Check
Point Declaration Immigration Interrogation
Intimidation – a sign – Do not Move Beyond
the Yellow Line, Do Not Sweat, Do Not Smile,
Do You Have Anything to Declare?

And for the longest time (one second and a half) I think.

I could declare my heart, my broken heart.
I could declare my feelings, my worn-out feelings.
I could declare that I left her, but I know
she left me.
I could declare my sadness, my complete sadness.
I could declare my anger, my old anger, my care.

Nothing, I say. *Nothing to declare.*

With steel eyes, he stamps my reason for entering Russia.
With downcast glances, I stamp my reason for leaving America
and walk ill hearted into realizing nothing
but the vastness of things unclaimed.

Enemies (A love story)

Along streets of long slow drowsy days
and nights of dazzling rain to a place
where I've lived on the surface of fears.

I was a child then, when the coast
of my Carolina city served homemade Russian missiles
for lunch at a cafe down the street.

Too young and too dark to eat at the counter
of a 1964 Dine 'N Five, I must've thought
the world was hinged on rubles wrapped
in the smoke laden smell of Soviet newspapers

announcing that the weather is changing its forecast
to the coldest war the world has yet seen.

And I in between the pages of Pushkin's fairy tales
slept soundly at night in my Carolina room. My days
spent cropping the bitter taste of Carolina tobacco.

At my Carolina dark school, my geography teacher said
Russia spans eleven time zones and at my early age
I felt the rage Carolina men held for the stage
of Mayakovsky's productions in black and white.

At the top of my voice, he said, and yes I
understood the simple reason for separation
in Carolina black and white people coming
and going no place unrecognized by lies
and the pale hard nature of the truth
promised me nothing out of the not so quite ordinary.

I took to the dictionary to find meaning and
there was none to explain cold war rain
that distorted the beauty of Carolina blue sky.

So I went to the cathedral of the Czars, had
lunch with the dead rulers of old Russia. Then
appeared out of the fog, thirty thousand feet over
the land, a man singing
renditions of *Midnight in Moscow,* and it took me
across the Sea of Japan toward Siberia into the sweetness
of Soviet science fiction and there I lived
for a while beneath my Carolina sun.

That doesn't mean I cried when Nikita died,
it doesn't mean I read Bulgakov or Chekhov more than one time,
it doesn't mean that my memory is unbelievably clear.

It simply means, as a child I heard the sounds
of moving water and came to love the smell
of St. Petersburg, the city of rivers, came to love
the names of sacred Soviet unpublished books,
and I came to love the vastness of Zhivago.

Moscow River

M I S S I S S I P P I, I learned the spelling of a river
before I learned my ABC's and I learned
that black and white are not colors before I learned
that primaries were

being held to inexact the Negro vote count long before.
I learned to count the letters in the British word COLOURED
(8) before I knew precisely what it meant to help

neighbors build bomb shelters in an effort to protect
them not us from red planes and red parachutes constructed
from muddy red Russian river water.

I knew how many dogs the Mississippi River Department
of Catch-A-Nigger had before I learned to tell the differences
between a Siberian Husky and a Siberian labor camp and
it wasn't hard to find the meaning of Moscow on a map
because I was the only one in first grade who didn't
take a nap on the lap of afternoons after recess.

My cold war dinners were always just beneath not-so-good
even when Grandmama did the best she possibly could
to warm our feelings in front of a pot belly wood burner
with sad eyes and a grin the size of anticipation
and preoccupation with the latest no-good news.

I knew her rheumatism came before Communism
in the backwards dictionary and it was never
out of the ordinary for me to bury my conceit
in the street and play football with white boys
whom I was not allowed to tackle but did
as a kid.

I knew that South Africa was in South Carolina,
that Indian was within the word of Indiana, that the Moscow River
flows into Jackson, Mississippi, and that I would grow up
and be the President of some-other-place because as a kid
I never did have enough American made anything
to be classified as such.

Red Love Note

Face to face one can't see the face.
Sergei Yesenin

Tragedy was her cousin and for a while,
at least, according to my recollections, they

were not close at all. So far away
she waited and wanted to be everything for me but

what I needed. Behind blue eyes she smiled often
before the storm of tide changings

brought to her shores too much wind and
too much rain. Life became sad for her

on the morning of my leaving for the sea
yet even then I can't say she understood

she was never to see the fatal beauty
of my pounding blue waves again.

All at once and almost without notice
I became the dance of a foreign sailor

spending foreign exchange, emphasizing
my complete unforgettable foreignness
in the sweet honey brown eyes of the exotic

south shore smiles and I was happy
at least, I thought until the note arrived

not in a bottle but by anchored ship mail
soaked not by the sea but by anchored ship rain.

It was then, at that swaying moment that I
remembered the poet's house by the sea-gate

and the unbearable white blinds
covering white painted windows in winter time.

I remembered Odessa in the summertime
of too many years and the thought of forgetfulness

reminded me all too carefully. I know love
and passion possess no tendency to violate.

Yet there was vivid violation, if in nothing more
than the swift sweet blow of careless wind

that somehow then seemed both kind and unkind
but unaware of the words either and neither.

Anyway, miles away, the same wind, jealous and unjealous,
delivered the note.

And I could not make out the rain soaked words
once, I suppose, so neatly printed on red unlined paper.

What she must have written was that love
is always tragedy like an unfamiliar ship

daring an uncharted sea like me, gone off course.
The wind and rain she must have known

can somehow chart the uncharted but
all too often they choose not to be concerned.

So jokingly, I leave without laughter to face
the impending, knowing tragedy is related to me also.

The Other Red Woman

(The Systematic Application of Pure Reason)

Like Copernicus who explained the movement of stars
by partly ascribing the movement of the observer,

if you are lucky enough to look closely enough

you can tell by the way the red lady sits,
legs crossed slightly beyond just enough

to demand complete attention to the necessary
all in the hollow span of a glance and nothing more.

Here at her table, coffee house cafe corner, she
often sits, reading a newly released novel slowly

the way a visitor from another country reads the legends
of a foreign city. The names of streets and avenues

not to be crossed, she knows the numbers and addresses
without looking both ways more than enough times.

What's to come—passionately peers. Dark becomes evening
suddenly on any restless moonless night. All scientific thinking

on the nature of this woman can be traced
to the distinctive geometric pattern formed by one star
in one sky. And she appears night after night

in precisely the same fixed position. I see

parts of her in my own frequency of this coffee smelling place.
Her face, not classic beauty but something more.

She is the profile of the *Portrait of a Lady,* somewhere
and everywhere at once in some other stray cabaret
reciting from memory

a poem, just audible enough to barely hear the words.
I make them out, each one, by studying her lips

the way Copernicus must have analyzed velocities
along the line of sight. Tonight
she sits in a chair so perfect, it was made for her
and she knows it without looking as if she knows

leaves fall in spring when she walks past trees.

Her hair is astrological, the wildest shade of red and yet
not quite so. A fatal delight. Her dress, always
a star fitting slender color

determined by the physics of lipstick outline and design

perfected in the discretion of long painted finger nails
wrapped carefully around a tall glass drink
mixed perfect as vodka and rocks in Moscow.

Yes, I know she has made a science out of waiting
for a man more married than I, more handsome
in his hand tailored handsome suit. And I know

what's to come peers passionately this restless moonless night.
All of this I know is predetermined cosmological doubt
but that's not what Copernicus was talking about.

Divided between an image I must've seen and an idea
I must've read in that same other novel, I light
my last cigarette, look for constellations and leave

the other red woman sitting in a chair so perfect,
it was made for her and she knows it.

Red

Paper
slow scatter beneath a red sun
in a red sky
then sets quietly over Red Square
which is neither
red nor square.

Red time knocks upon a red door
to share the red evening
over red tea.
Too much has passed of late and
goes unrecognized.
The evolution of revolution keeps turning
out dead red poets of unbelievable promise.

In a red room we sit in red 1917 drinking
red wine and know, we know
that labels on bottles
lie to get at the truth. Some among us call it
the larger truth,
but how can that be.
Truth is not large or small.
Truth is red

like dead carnations, tulips, buses,
cars, people
who all smile at themselves
in red mirrors that reflect
this red city. Red birds, red cowards, red warnings,
red morning
over Red Square which is neither red
nor square.
Red Jesus, red hello, red you know, red promise,
red sign stop.

Now start again, red live music, red dance,
red head lady,
red dress, red tall shoes, red news
paper.

The Girl

(Once I saw Marina 1892-1941)

On the morning she was born a rose colored sun
rose empty and early, not quite to an ordinary world.

She was the girl for not so long, the people had waited
and wanted her to be their Tsvetaeva. The people needed

a writer in the family, a mirrored dance maker
in the ballet room. They needed a girl with the look

of a czarina in times when wild strawberries, the sweetest
of their wild forest fruit had dearly forgotten

to grow thickly along edges of abandoned outreaching fields.

On the morning she was born divine St. John christened
the water with sugar as the afternoon of her birth fell
upon itself.

Leaves began to tremble in birch trees as if before
a wind storm, as if they knew the terrible results
of resentment.

As if the girl, herself, knew her role, her lines so well
appearance at casting call was not necessary. A play maker
for the dance maker of words sealed

in an envelope was the poet's first prize. The girl
she never wanted to be fated in the dull
red blueness of orange red October history. She wanted

logic not tragic magic realism. Married early like the sun
she and Sergei lived first in Prague then Paris

exiled in extreme poverty in extreme strange places,
one gloomy suburb to another. Extremely saddened

by and in the shadows of foreign gaiety and glamor,
the slate smell of raids in the air everywhere.

The girl never wanted to be the mother of a son killed

in the first weeks of war. The girl never wanted to be
the mother of a daughter sent to a concentration camp for nothing
beyond the ordinary. The girl wanted

logic in the oil lamp light to flicker at night
in one room long enough to be called home.

But August '41 proved more tragic than Paris,
more tragic than Prague. She forgot

she was born to listen to the rose colored sun.

I met the girl first in 1923, the aftermath of Revolution
was forcing writers to leave. It was at Yaroslavsky station.

The girl was headed for Prague. She had almost no luggage,
Sergei walked ahead, their daughter paced behind.

The girl was wearing massive silver rings.
There was a flare at the hem of her strawberry skirt.

As to a cloud and not the rose colored sun, she said,
In this bedlam of nonpeople I refuse to be alive.

The Boy

Once I saw Vladimir (1893-1930)

On the night he was born the moon was full
of purple sweet joy. He was the boy

for so long the people had waited and they wanted
the boy to be their Mayakovsky. They needed

a writer in the family, a weathermaker
in the drawing room. They needed a boy with the look

of a czar in times when hungry weeds grew
with bad reason in the Summer Palace garden. On the night

he was born, they were happy as happiness upon arrival
after a long journey or upon receiving an unexpected letter

from a friend not heard from in years. Suddenly
like the slate smell of dry desert rain, rejoice persuaded
the voices

to sing and that night the moon and all of her sisters
were full of purple sweet joy. The boy had arrived
in light of an odd shaped hue.

The few who knew did not mention the coming of madness.

Thirteen years would pass before the boy realized that
his eyes were not blue, not green but something in between

what could never be a serene and tranquil life beyond
that fated red faded October history. The boy
never wanted to be Mayakovsky. He wanted magic

to appear out of the Moscow fog. Resentment more than not
has terrible unforgiving results. The moon always loses
in its fight with the stars of the dipper. The boy,

too soon he was arrested, too soon a year in prison,
too soon a poet of instant fame at 18, too soon the light
faded to black. The stage of the *Bedbug* went empty and silent.

The boy, once I saw him, I did not speak to the boy.
The boy did not speak to me. Once I heard a shot
ring out into the coolness of the morning. The boy,

he never wanted to be Mayakovsky. He never wanted to write
The Last Pages of the Civil War. The boy simply wanted to live

in pages new and freshly remembered. Reason forgives
but forgets everything. The boy did not speak to me.

Korolenko Prospekt

I would have thought it a ridiculous thing to say
but I said it anyway. I'll live with it.

She, I must explain, was not first in my life at the time.
Sometimes I question if even she were second. Anyway

for a time she was there beside me in that sacred room
on the third floor on Korolenko Prospekt. For a time

she held me as tender as I would allow. Perhaps
it was because my mind was elsewhere most of the time

and often I paid little attention to the routine of
every now and then, then again it could've been

that at the time I was unable to love anyone else
and my feelings were so far away from anything easily

explainable but that's another story or maybe it's the same
old story: A boy wants what he no longer has. Sveta, she

loved me when she loved me and for a while I knew heaven
in the greenness of her eyes, then one morning she left.

Bella lived next door. At first, one night then another
until she came to live in my sacred room on Korolenko Prospekt.

It was Bella that I learned to love but that was before
the postcard arrived. It was a simple postcard.

It mentioned nothing about love but her name
was on it. I loved the way Sveta signed her name, the

simple grace of the letters as they curved around
each other to form the memory of perfect

evenings where candlelight danced in the reflection
of our eyes. White wine and fireplaces, soft heat

fanning faces. It was a simple postcard with a
simple stamp, with a simple picture of simple spring

flowers on the front. It mentioned nothing about love.
I would've thought it was a ridiculous thing to say.

Bella said she understood. It's been two years and
I still don't. Stubbornly, without love, I now live
between that and this and then and there, in my room
on Korolenko Prospekt. Bella sleeps so soundlessly.

In This Room

Immanuel Kant (1724-1804)

They say along this road, every day he walked
so punctual, people set time to the ticks of his steps.

I say tree stained glass cathedral windows cast
rainbows across his westside gravesite.

They say this place was built in 1333, September 13,
and burned by bombs in 1944.

I say the birch trees of spring lay lightly
against the blue sky in July.

They say he lectured his philosophy here in this room
for everyone who wanted to listen.

I say the trees, it seems, have been forced to face
west toward Germany.

They say Kaliningrad was Koenigsberg then,
a town in East Prussia.

I say I always found my sacredness in the sweetness
of sacred gum trees.

They say he was not handsome, scarcely five feet tall,
but women loved him and he loved them back.

I say I slept in a bed of oak tree moss
when I was little, I am told.

They say the burning of this room was hotter
than the sun and German children burned in this room.

I say the forest kept their promise and never harmed
my childhood trees.

They say he was forbidden in 1793 to lecture or write
further on subjects of religion.

I say here I find the slow dance of birch trees
simply amazing.

They say he returned to the subject, in spite of himself,
in his last essay.

I say the leaves of trees have always
caused me to listen much too carefully.

They say his *The Critique of Pure Reason* was the result
of 10 years of meditation.

I say how green my valley would not be
without the hurriedness of trees.

They say for the children of '44, one candle
now burns in this room.

I say for a philosopher and for a tree, for you
Russian nun lady and for me.

Reframing the Market Place Dog

No one tells them what to think so they, the dogs,
think of themselves as humans.
Everyone tells them what to think so they, the humans,
think of themselves as dogs.

Saturday morning at the market brews like a storm
twisting and turning rage into second hand rags
draped raggedly across the shoulders of Gypsy beggars

who've dyed their hair blond as if to fool someone,
anyone, everyone into giving more than one
or two Kopecks to the smallest of the Gypsy daughters
holding tightly to Gypsy mother's hand

comparing the smell of raw meat hanging from hooks
that kills men but makes a dog very happy. Fish,
the smell of, dried, nasty, permeates everything.

Apples and oranges and grapes taste of the smell.
The dogs, no one tells them what to think,
so they roam as gentlemen without obligation. The men
having been told, lick and laugh and salivate
until the whole of the market place floor is wet

and alive with ceaseless chatter and fresh baked bread
dead waiting to be sliced or torn apart then licked up,
every crumb, by the slicer. And who is to say
what's happening here.

The dogs sit and watch and are amazed
that men not only take great pleasure
in devouring other men's spirits, but also
in the eating of other men's bones. And I

the observer of all of this take one picture out
of one frame and replace it with another.

Separated City

(Kaliningrad)

I've counted 17 dogs this morning. All coming
from the same unknown direction. An orange Lada,
as old as three decades, drives by. In the East

tulips are in much needed bloom. I stand
at the window of a crowdedly furnished room
two stories above the rush. It's Saturday early

and already Pavlo is standing up, leaning drunk,

but I do not blame him. He blames himself
for the state of things, the price of bread
and meat. He lives not in the street, but
in a cellar, a wine cellar.

On Pavlo's street bus riders wait on benches
painted yellow and blue. Bicycle riders ride by
one by one and two by two. Koenigsburg was the name
when Germany was here. Now only the bitter taste of stout
is left in the bottom of glasses on tables at streetside patios

and outside cafes. Pavlo preaches to himself.

There are few street signs. You know or you don't.
Morning newspaper readers wait for the cable car bus.
Out into the blanket breeze, a Bible man strolls
carrying his Jesus as one would carry a jacket
in the heat of the day, loosely.

In this city separated, Pavlo walks the same line
as the Bible man, that line that divides
the poor from the poorer from the poorest people
these unnamed streets afford.

Pure white they paint the bottom of tree trunks
for decoration, for observation, for something
untranslatable. Make no mistake. Pavlo eats well.

There is meat, good meat at the market, but
he prefers to drink the entirety of his atmosphere
instead. Like a little kid, he lives for a good time.

Another dog. That makes 18. Somewhere in the distance
a cat or a woman or maybe it's Pavlo who yells out
to all of Germany, *Give back to me my city.*

Upstairs two stories above the noise I shut
the window and turn the dial to Radio Free Pavlo.
Slowly, I'm learning to understand the language
of 18 dogs who move unaffected by the absence
of street signs in this unnamed separated city.

Sweeping Dirt

For the lady I saw

Perhaps she remembers, perhaps they all remember
when all of Russia was red dirt. Perhaps
I should close the window

to this third floor room, but I won't, not yet,
it's too hot in Kaliningrad this morning. So I look
out into the breeze, onto the intersection where

all things come together, where four dirt streets meet,
where the lady has been sweeping and sweeping until
they appear almost paved.

The lady, she wears black tall rubber boots and a skirt
that flares so that the tops are invisible. Her head
is covered by a rag tied unproud around
what is necessary. She is in no hurry.

Cars, they come, stop and go as if to give moments
of dirt contemplation. Diligently the sweeper sweeps
small piles of morning from center to sides.

The dogs, they come, stop and go as if to investigate
without looking up at me sitting here holding a fork
and a knife and a voice of my own appointment, eating

caviar for breakfast from a plastic plate. Drinking vodka for milk.
I should be happy and I am
so far away from home until small things

like sweeping dirt simply amaze me. Perhaps
it reminds me of my childhood, a little boy growing up
in North Carolina living in dirt. Dirt front yard, dirt
back porch, dirt always on the kitchen floor.

Oh how we paid for the dirt that gave permission to live
and oh how happy we lived in that dirt. Sometimes
I can still hear my grandmama saying, *Boy, go out there
and sweep the dirt.*

As a child I hated yard brooms and hound dogs
we seemed always to have that just laid there in the yard
at the edge and just watched dirt rise and fall

stubborn and determined as any dirt this morning in this city.
I look down, three stories above dirt. I've finished my milk.
It's getting late. Tiny black specks left on a white plastic plate.

Perhaps I should button up my shirt, go down to the street
and tell that lady that I remember all
too well what I wish I would forget.

Warsaw Seesaw

(Unfolding the unforgettable)

I see Warsaw when, perhaps, Warsaw
does not see me in this city refreshed

by insights, I've lately attempted to lay aside.

As in lately, I've come to know the pain
of being broken into too many directions.

War and Peace are names given to rival rivers
and a hard bumpynight road divides
my crime from my punishment.

And in this city
I've lately come, people divide from people
with the kind of slow ease to please

the subtle movement of layout and maps
neither of which I'm able to read.

Need is what I do not need. I have enough to last
forever it seems I stand waiting and watching

for a city street crowded bus among worlds
of paper white leg girls and Polish school boys

going to and coming from places kind and unkind.

Here in this city where men and women do not speak,
nod, or acknowledge this American dreamer dreaming

solo along these rambling insane streets of seduction.

Yes, I have been seduced by such no whereness, such an
ignorant arrangement of unpronounceable avenues

and streets that eat their own white lines.
Here in this city the lost has become more so.

Yet there is a beauty in decay of an empty
forgotten day without plan or promise or premise

just an all too imposing sun all too hot and bright.

Bring on the night. The waiters wait. No bus
in sight. A brown borrowedness covers my skin
tenderly enough to smooth the rough perceptions

of things both named and unnamed, things
both unforgivable and unforgettable in combinations
of pride and doom. I see Warsaw

when it does not see me ambling toward
my clear unfocused purpose, wearing my sad silk

shirt of protection, rejection, perfection
in its simple oversize fit

into the wide empty days when I speak about
everything except what should be said about

the deadening sense of what I now feel. It should be
said, I loved her beyond the borders of this,
another country.

But empty days are not really empty. In these alley ways

cars and cares fly by like airplanes leaving long sad lines
across an unscattered sky and I could leave

on a jet plane to some other place, unpleased by the lack
of simple Polish pleasure. Yet

my war is here, my peace, my crime,
my punishment, my lost love. All filed under
Fold, forget, and go. But I refuse such

simple solutions. Here, now, I stand waiting
for a simple crowded street city bus to take me

deeper into the strong swift city currents

where I shall be pushed aside from everything
slowly toward what's been needed.

All morning I have worked not to remember things
and it is now early afternoon. Soon the crowds

will leave me alone in my sad confusion of layouts

and maps. Neither of which I'm able to read.

Need is a seed that germinates and grows wildly
into the folds of the unplanned and unpromised

sight of a bus that finally comes crowded
to take me into her arms. She is beautiful. For a while, I'll
ease into the pleasure of standing up for what

I no longer stand for.

On the Other End

of a bench I sit opposite
an old Russian man wearing a seafarer hat
though we, two, are years and miles
from the sea.

He eats me as he eats peanuts, tossing shells,
some toward me, some away. I read
Akhmatova aloud low to myself. People

walk by, going to and coming from places.
I see their end-of-the-workday faces
pleased not to be going in whichever is
the other way.

No one speaks, not even the peanut shell man
in his down and up coat, his outgoing boots
and his contained, buttoned-to-the-very-top shirt
of too many unremarkable patterns and prints
and perfect unfit weather proofness.

Spring, here, is trying to break. Yesterday
was almost unholy hot. Today is a cool overcast
with an expectation of light to medium rain.
I forgot to bring a jacket. I feel so alone. Time
seems so desolate and weak.

Sadly, I cross my legs and watch the movement,
the uniformed gait of masses. The old man
is now gone to another bench in another park
I suppose. A bus rumbles by then another.

I haven't seen any dogs today. Perhaps
it's a holiday and they all, somewhere, celebrate.
More crowds gather at bus stops and wait.

On the other end, a lady takes what used to be
an old man's seat. I read Akhmatova loud low to myself.

The lady smokes. She doesn't speak.
Kids! Three surround her, talking all at once
but taking turns, one by one, to watch me

an American Negro taking not so great care
not to stare at the beautiful hair on the legs
of the cigarette lady on the other end
of everything I came to this place to find.

A Gathering of Old Russian Men

(Just another day at the park)

Every day they sit around a picnic table
in a dirt park filled with too much maple leaf shade
and talk

I suppose about how things used to be or how things
ought to be or perhaps how things are. Anyway
today is May 9th, Victory Day in all of Russia.

Each is adorned in war decorations, each wears
them proudly and each swaps the story of his private war.

Standing at this window looking down, I know they know
every man's story by heart. But it's not the heart
that matters, it's the medals, the magic of medals.

These are the strong, young, brave boys of the Red Army
of 1944. These are the soldiers who scared
America into building bomb shelters during the 50's
Red Scare and these are the young lovers who left lovers
at home to step so proudly for Stalin and Kruschev.
These are the ones who shined their boots with rags
of America, who goose stepped higher than Nazi Germany.

These, now, old Russian men gloriously turn into twilight
under a maple shade tree in a dirt park. Chess in the park
is the war they now fight and they've come gallantly
decorated to win.

December Remembers Nothing

There's a seductiveness about memory that can
Leave reality looking quite pale.
                    Dominique Browning

In this aggressive atmosphere, observation grows keen
to the exhaustive analysis of traces in the faces
of hat and shoes that have become metaphors

for philosophical contemplation about the way life was
before October. This is what I remember.

On the morning of my leaving Kharkov, I returned
to my bench in the park. Signs of spring were in everything.
The dark of winter clothes   slowly changed
to a lighter shade of darkness, a lighter shade
of unsacred black.

The pace of walkers   slowed to an even, warm stroll.
Young and old removed weather beaten hands from pockets
of cold war coats. Poplar trees promised green sunshine
and birch trees gave way to white light.

Spring had come to save these paper plastic bag people
who live in this city of rage rumbling motor cars and
trucks that do not   slow for old ladies crossing and
buses fight to ride one more rider beyond the overcrowded.

Today is looking toward May and all of the city, it seems,
is praying winter's over. On my bench I turn
to face myself and wonder why December remembers nothing
and I almost everything.

Rock Russia Roll

For her

Thomas Earl Petty and the Heartbreakers live
on stage in a room spinning on a turning table.
Don't have to live like a refugee,

belting out at the top of his voice an *American Girl*
in Moscow. A party for me, an American boy in Levis.

Sheryl Crow spins around and turns that CD player
the otherside down. She's *Leaving Las Vegas* for the first
and last time. I am leaving Russia with a shot of vodka
in my hand. Eric Clapton and his band pops in and breaks down
you look *Wonderful Tonight.*

And she is looking wonderful tonight but I am feeling
just a bit better than. Someone threw on Van "the Man" Morrison
Into the Mystic and Welsh Witch Stevie Nicks dances in
outa the fog. An American girl in Moscow waltzes with me

hot and slow like syrup in Miles Davis' mixed up maxed out bitches brew.
We knew morning in Moscow would never come. But Queen
without the machine takes us in. Freddie Mercury is dead

ahead and Curtis "Superfly" Mayfield is prancing and strutting
in one of his famous yellow suits. Roll out the Rolling Stones.

Crazy Mick Jagger drunk but not as drunk as Ronnie Wood, drunk
but not as drunk as Keith Richards, drunk and playing guitar
like it's "1999" and the Purple Prince of rain is looking for the Police

to come calling at any time. Sting is singing everything.
Every breath you take we take 'til there is no breathing room
in the room. Nothing but smoke folded into the arms
of that satisfaction song. I can't get none

and we don't want any. We have plenty to roll
'til we can barely see Jackson Browne *Doctor my eyes.*

Someone tells someone to call one. Doctor John, Doctor Hook
not on call tonight. The Beach Boys show up minus one Brian Wilson

Pickett "Mustang Sally" you better slow that mustang down.
Rod Stewart couldn't do it. Rickie Lee Jones couldn't do it.
Tina "Turn Around" Turner could not do it.

We couldn't do it and we don't even try. We are
higher than Sly and the Family Stone seven time zones
away from home, me and an American girl in Moscow.

Yes, all of this on my last night in town. All of this,
the music, the madness, the Soviet missile made sadness
wrapped, bowed and ribboned red second place
for me. Don't ya boy mess around with no cigarette trash.
When in Russia, Kopecks and Rubles ain't good as good ole
American cash. I'll be broke by day break.

Jim, Janis, and Jimi on the stereo replaced
by one big fat boy named Meatloaf and Jerry Lee Lewis
is still the only one capable of making a piano jump
completely off the stage-rage in the room.

Ziggy Stardust is dead, the Thin White Duke is dead,
John Lennon is dead, the Big Bopper is dead,
Elvis was dead, the Grateful Dead is dead, Keith Moon is dead
but the drums are still playing loud as the Who

are you and what are you and that girl doing here
in this Saturday night room full of smoke and matches
and ashes and oil scented to smell like hell and Heaven
and everything there might be in between the two?

Who are you? I'm Neil "Crazy Horse" Young
Down by the River looking for a *Cowgirl in the Sand*.

I'm the Clash like lightning, the Raincoats like a storm,
the New York City Dolls back in 1973. I am me Bruce Hornsby
and Brian Setzer *Jump, Jive, and Wail.* I am Bob Dylan
and John Cougar Mellencamp. I'm Jack and I am Diane.

I am *Back in USSR, boy you don't know how lucky you are*
to be so far away from the place that slapped you
in your black face. Sing the blues boy. Rock'n Roll is white

but not tonight soundlessly I sleep with an American girl
in Moscow. I'm the Best of Bruce Springsteen. The best
of the "Boss." I was *Born in the USA.* Turn out the lights

my darling, play some Marvin Gaye. *Let's get it on*
before the rains come and wash the night away. Play it
sweetheart, play some Marvin Gaye. Play it girl, play
some Marvin Gaye, soft and slow 'til we know
the meaning of love.

Upon My Return from Russia, Memorial Day Morning

(5 a.m. in New Haven)

On a stage of ghosts and shadow dancers
I danced, last night, into this town.

I have studied the science of leaving cities behind.
I have given to letting the names define themselves.

New Haven is not new at all but that's another story.
This morning while the outskirts pretend to sleep

I keep busy wrapping my fear in brown paper, sitting here
at curbside, I wait for jet lag to subside, I wait

for a ride to take me away from the hardness of Russia
still ever present in my mind. But I was afraid then

when border guards and border patrols searched
my essence to a fault and blamed me for everything

they could not find. My passport was a report
card in elementary education with all failing grades.

Yet I passed through checkpoint after checkpoint,
checked and pointed at by a machine gun, indirectly, of course.

But I was shot in the heart of my own madness
in that place where sadness and happiness are sisters

with the same features as Yevtushenko said,
I have studied the science of leaving cities behind.

Like green is the perfect color for painting summer leaves
this place is perfect for contemplation and observation.

The sky is azure without clouds, birds sing
and fly by like unattached flags — waves of color.

Naked light poles now without light stand and wait
for the valuable night, pointing toward unvast emptiness.

From this vantage point I think of you and see my life
written on four street signs: No Left Turn, One Way,

Do Not Enter and No Parking Zone. Only a few days ago
I was eight time zones away from this no parking space.

It was raining in all of Russia and I was going along
crowded Moscow streets in nights of Moscow dreams

And you were there in your wild wide wicked lovable way
savoring every day as though it were the last

or the first. It's so hard to tell when suspicion
knows exactly who you are and exactly why you cry

in the streets of wide openness. This morning, I'm the only one
awake in the world, it seems. It's celebration day,

Memorial Day, a day of respect for dead uniforms. All is quiet now
but by 10 o'clock someone will strike up the band

and I will hear the little drummer boys
and girls marching for mercy, blowing horns,

throwing batons—catching most but missing some.
By early afternoon the red hot grills will be ready

and the hamburgers will flip themselves. The smell
of barbecue will beckon the hungry from games

of frisbee and horse shoe. Children will play
as only children can and a man with no home

will come uninvited to supper and he will be given every course
of the celebrated however many course meal.

He will proclaim loudly for everyone to hear
I was killed seven times in Vietnam for no Medal of Honor.

Everyone will eat together and enjoy it for the dead uniforms.
Afterwards, the young boys will line up the night

saying, *Come here girl, you are finer than Nappa Valley Zinfandel.*
Dogs, too, will beg because that's what dogs do and I

will think of you while stray cats creep to keep
from being recognized eight time zones away

clawing at windows trying to see inside. And what am I
doing here in New Haven in the morning sitting at curbside?

As my grandmama used to say when I asked her,
why the beauty of the full moon so quickly covered herself

in the ugliness of clouds? *Ask me no questions,* she said,
and I will tell you no lies.

I was always surprised and I still am as I remember
the thinness of things unnamed, but clearly recognized.

Vladivostok

for Osip Emilievich Mandelstam

In Russia all things begin in Moscow but
only migrating birds know all things end in Vladivostok,
7 time zones east on the Sea of Japan.

The longest railway in the world stops here,
the Trans-Siberian Express.

6 encumbered days, 12 uninvited hours, and 25 dead minutes
from the point of embark, I, the American blue stranger,
disembark

into an ocean of stiff morning-grey uniforms
strategically faced amid masses of unmatched salty Russian fish-
ermen and women dressed in dead winter beige. No street here

is better than any other. There's a sad ugly kindness in the air.
This city, surrounded by water and rolling hills,
from a distance, charming as any San Francisco
but I know the difference.

Svetlanskaya Cafe located exactly on Svetlanskaya Street.
Too dreary and too cold to eat, I stand at the corner
of this and that street forgetting and remembering
the train window view

through the town of 2 "Secret Cities" unmarked
on Soviet era maps and pointed caps of station guard rifles,
the town of 2 vodka bottles unlabeled in the middle
of a Soviet make-shake table, the town of 2 hundred million

birch trees counting us as we passed, unimpressed
by Soviet train speed, the town of too many

long faces in places unannounced thus unnamed in the voice
of Soviet conductors conducting ornithology classes
through the town of 2 thousand mountain ranges unprepared

for what seemed like one Soviet station change after another.
And then there was the town of 2 men in my cabin
unable to move

beyond the scope of logic, classic Soviet style logic, so I
forgot and they, always a Victor, always a Nikolai, forgave
me for requesting the clearest view, a window seat

facing backwards, looking into the past. 1938.
From a shot in a small glass vodka corner, I saw it all
on the bank of the Second River, a transit camp. This city
killed Osip. I slip when I step into this city
salty like dried fish sleeping now so unconcerned,
twisting without turning on a bed of Asian rice. This city.

Osip, killed for writing a poem. It was a simple poem
about whoever finds the horseshoe, a poem without paragraphs.

Between this and that, no street here is better
than any other. Between a lookup and a lookdown,
I look around.

What once was proud and tall has fallen down, Lenin,
Stalin, the Kremlin now covered by the green and white
of migrating birds.

Gazing window, not quite red, not quite square, upon yellow stucco
seem not to know they too are guilty. Oh how I wish I could dance
in the streets

of this salt city, the city that killed Osip, but
I hear no music here. Yes, I know it would be good
to dress myself handsome in Lord Byron's poet shirt
with cuffs undone at center stage.

Like a little kid I wish I could be Baryshnikov dancing
a ballet back to Boston, but I hear no music here

in this city that killed Osip. This tired strange salty Siberian city
where no street is better than any other, where no one seems
to remember, this city where the end of the line
is the end of the line.

About the Author

Earl S. Braggs, UC Foundation Associate Professor of English at the University of Tennessee at Chattanooga, is the author of *Hat Dancer Blue*, winner of the 1992 Anhinga Prize selected by Marvin Bell, and *Walking Back from Woodstock*. "After Allyson," a chapter from his novel in progress, *Looking for Jack Kerouac*, won the 1995 Jack Kerouac Literary Prize. Supported with a summer fellowship from the University of Tennessee at Chattanooga, he traveled in Russia in 1998.

7270

AEI-2879

Gramley Library
Salem Academy and College
Winston-Salem, N.C. 27108